The Crystal Palace High Level Railway

by John Gale

The Crystal Palace tram terminal was situated at the top of Anerley Hill, near to the High Level station, although there are directions to the LB&SCR station offering 'electric trains to London'. That company had introduced electric services to Victoria in May 1911. However, cheap tram fares took passengers away from the railways. *Pamlin Prints*

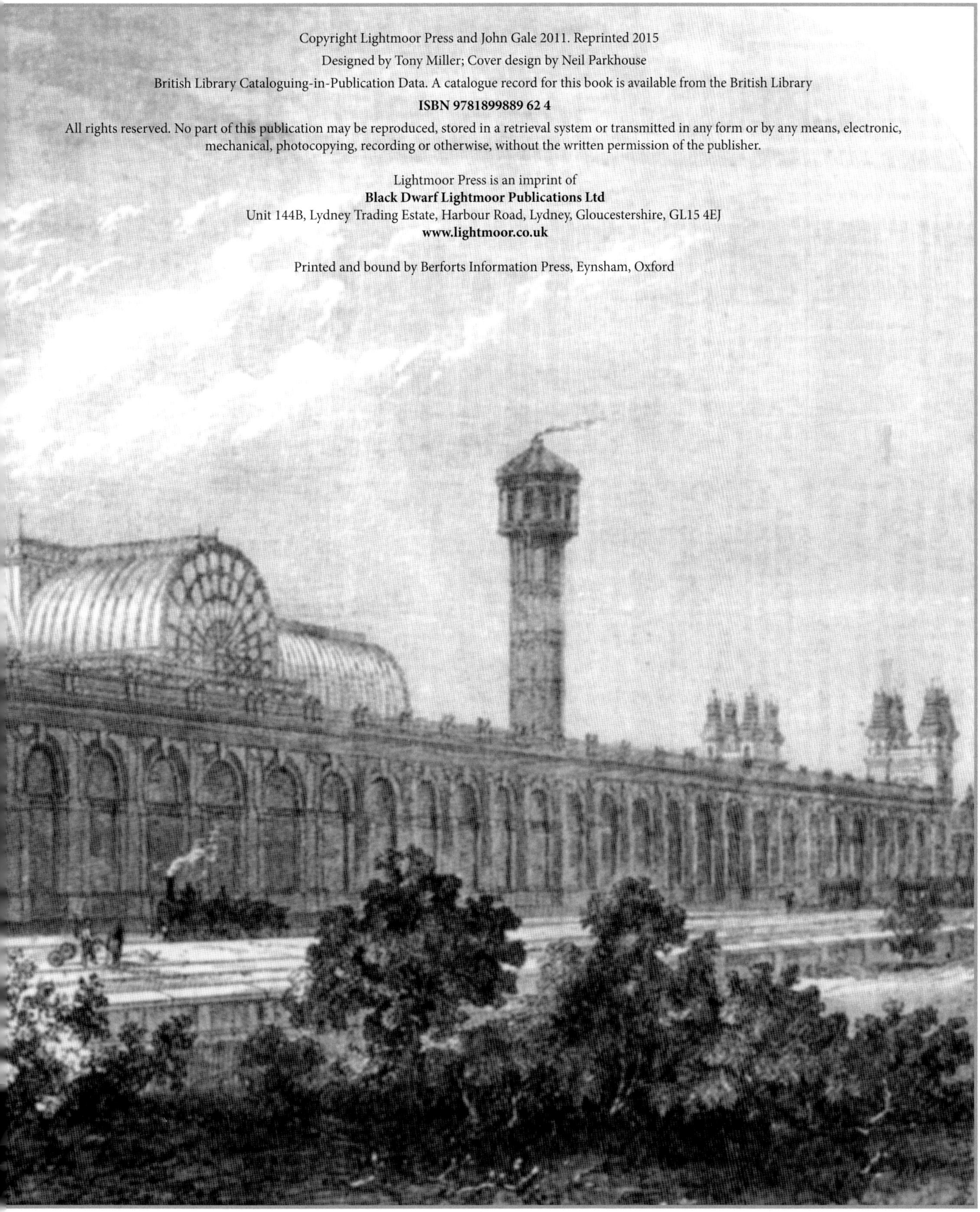

Copyright Lightmoor Press and John Gale 2011. Reprinted 2015

Designed by Tony Miller; Cover design by Neil Parkhouse

British Library Cataloguing-in-Publication Data. A catalogue record for this book is available from the British Library

ISBN 9781899889 62 4

Lightmoor Press is an imprint of
Black Dwarf Lightmoor Publications Ltd
Unit 144B, Lydney Trading Estate, Harbour Road, Lydney, Gloucestershire, GL15 4EJ
www.lightmoor.co.uk

Printed and bound by Berforts Information Press, Eynsham, Oxford

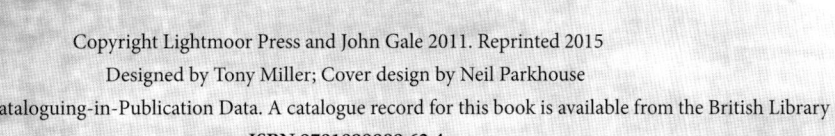

❀ CONTENTS ❀

Frontispiece - *previous page*

The Frontispiece is from an engraving that was published in the *Illustrated London News* on 30th September 1865. The ornate High Level station is dominated by the Crystal Palace itself but was connected to the exhibition halls by a subway under Crystal Palace Parade, which ran between the station and the Crystal Palace. Nominally built by the Crystal Palace & South London Junction Railway, that company had been the brainchild of the London, Chatham & Dover Railway who espied an opportunity to, firstly, connect the area to the City and, secondly, share in the lucrative traffic as visitors came to visit the Palace and its attractions.

Depicted some two months after its opening, the station layout was enlarged during its lifetime and was gradually equipped with more sophisticated signalling compared with the signalling hut to the left of the picture. The 2-2-2 locomotives purchased by the LC&DR and shown in the engraving were not up to the job and were replaced by 0-4-2 tank engines. See also *Plate 6*.

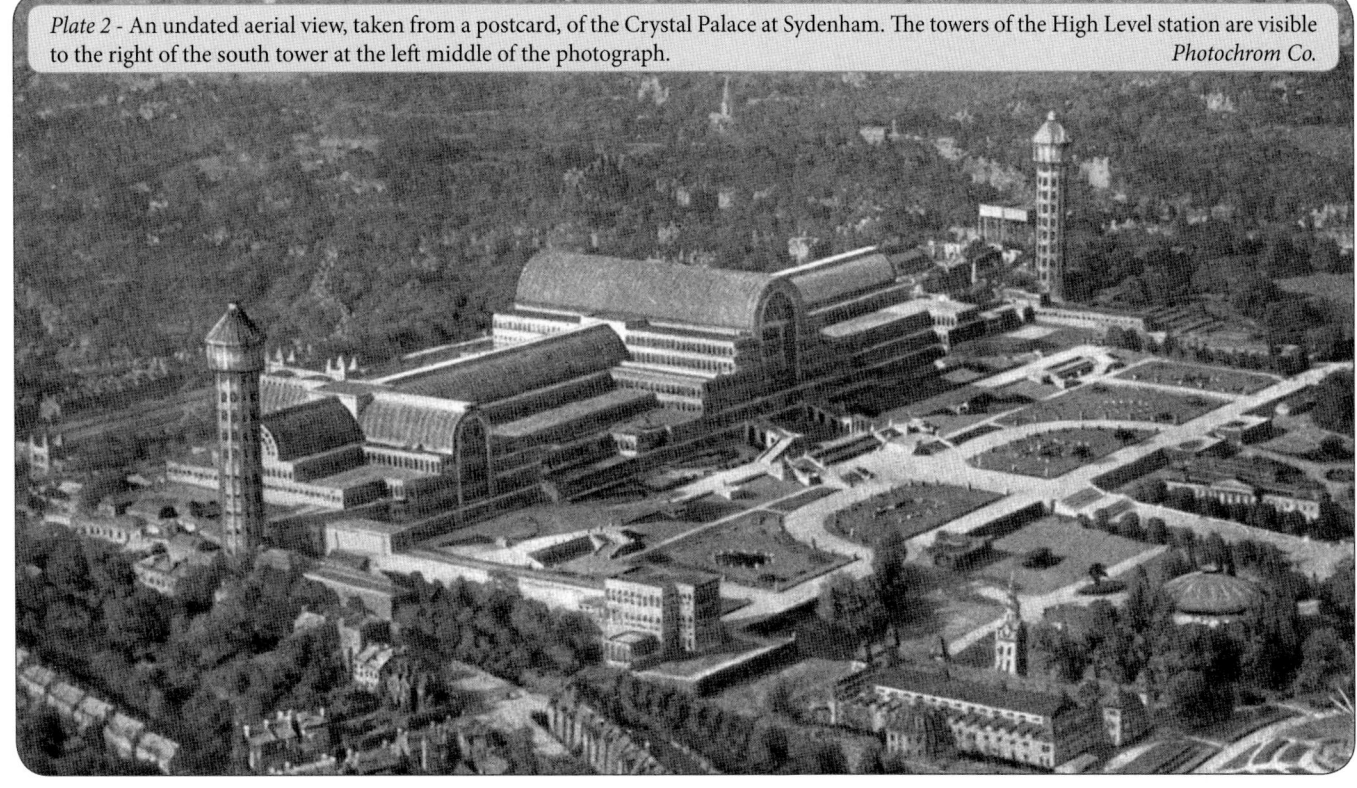

Plate 2 - An undated aerial view, taken from a postcard, of the Crystal Palace at Sydenham. The towers of the High Level station are visible to the right of the south tower at the left middle of the photograph.

Photochrom Co.

❈ *Introduction* ❈

'A palace of glass to provide pleasure and education for the working classes.'

Joseph Paxton's Crystal Palace, erected on the downs at Sydenham in 1854, attracted visitors in their thousands for over eighty-two years. A structure unprecedented at the time, and set in magnificent grounds, the building captured the spirit of the Victorian age. Its popularity ensured a constant flow of visitors, and there is no doubt that the presence of the Palace greatly assisted the development of Sydenham and the surrounding area.

The nineteenth century was the age of the railway speculator, and the new Crystal Palace offered a unique opportunity to reap vast profits. It is therefore not surprising that competing railway companies should have constructed lines to the Palace in order to profit from what appeared to be a never ending supply of passengers. The London, Brighton & South Coast Railway was successful in this venture, carrying over ten thousand passengers daily in its heyday to the Crystal Palace Low Level station, and this success is marked by the fact that the line continues in use to the present day. The High Level line, however, terminated at the Crystal Palace and was never able to expand. Although relatively successful in its early years, successive railway companies failed to make the line profitable, and consequently it was closed in 1954.

This book is primarily concerned with the formation of the Crystal Palace & South London Junction Railway and the subsequent history of its High Level line, which ran between the terminus at Crystal Palace and Nunhead station. The line proved difficult to construct, being carried out mostly in cuttings, tunnels or on embankments, and despite the grandeur of the Crystal Palace High Level station which cost £100,000, the line was always operated on a shoestring budget.

Much of the information given in the book is in the form of quotations taken from local newspapers stored in the archives of Bromley, Croydon, Southwark, Lambeth, Lewisham and Upper Norwood libraries. The National Archives at Kew has also been a further source of information. There are also a number of books and periodicals which provide details of the Crystal Palace railways, and these have proved to be invaluable.

Two national newspapers, *The Times*, (Copyright NI Syndication, London) and the *Daily Herald* (now the *Sun*) have been quoted in connection with the closure of the line in 1954. Details of the controversy surrounding the Camille Pissarro picture of Lordship Lane station in 1977 were also obtained from *The Times*, London.

Permission to use photographs has kindly been given by the London Metropolitan Archives, the National Railway Museum, Ashford Local Studies Library, Lambeth Local Studies Library, Southwark Local Studies Library, the Mike Morant Collection, The Transport Treasury, the Courtauld Institute, Dulwich College, the Crystal Palace Museum, Pamlin Prints, Roger Carpenter, John Alsop and Lens of Sutton Association.

Plate 3 - The Crystal Palace at Sydenham on an unspecified date. The Palace is obviously the main subject of the photographer's interest since he has managed to photograph it as the sun peeps through the clouds, illuminating the exhibition halls and the gardens to the right. Unfortunately, this leaves the High Level station in some cloud shadow.

The main exhibition halls and galleries of the Crystal Palace are prominent in the centre with the two water structures towering over the north and south ends. The layout of the gardens is quite clear. To the left of the Crystal Palace buildings is The Parade, running from bottom to upper middle of the picture. Further to the left of The Parade is the High Level station, at a lower level than The Parade and protected by a high retaining wall, as will be seen in photographs later in this book.

It is tempting to interpret the long pale strips of the station as platforms but that is not so; they are parts of the overall roof structures. The railway line from Nunhead is carried through Paxton Tunnel at the far right-hand corner of the station site and the two tracks fan out to provide four platform lines and a long headshunt outside the left-hand wall of the station. The head-shunt affords access to the storage sidings - the rake of pale-roofed vehicles is stabled in one of those sidings - and a coal yard at the extreme left of the station site with access from Farquhar Road. There are two additional storage sidings at the extreme right of the site against the retaining wall. They are both occupied by what appears to be electric train units; the white headcode panels are readily visible when the photograph is enlarged.

Farquhar Road is the road to the left of the station site and is the one flanked by a terrace of high-rise buildings which describe a backward-written 'S'. It curves sharply to pass in front of the twin towers of the High Level station and, at the same time, it is bridging the extended platform lines that give access to the turntable which had been installed to allow release of the locomotives of incoming trains.

There was pedestrian access to the station from The Parade and, for first class passengers in the heyday of the Crystal Palace, a separate subway led directly from the station, under The Parade and into the Crystal Palace itself. Money had its privileges!

Photograph courtesy Ian Pope

❧ *Chapter One* ❧

PAXTON'S PALACE

The Great Exhibition held in Hyde Park in 1851 was organised by a Royal Commission headed by Prince Albert, and lasted for one hundred and forty-four days. The objective of the exhibition was to highlight the achievements of the Industrial Revolution; however, it was hoped that it would also serve as a cultural activity for the education of the masses. Preparatory works took less than fifteen months, and during the period of its opening 6,170,000[1] people visited the newly erected glass structure designed by Joseph Paxton, the Duke of Devonshire's head gardener. They were able to view a variety of exhibits which were considered by some to be useful and elegant, and by others to be ridiculous and tasteless. More recently the exhibits have been described as '... the most incredible collection of unsorted junk ever assembled.' [2]

Despite the controversial nature of the work submitted by over 17,000 exhibitors, the Great Exhibition was an outstanding success. Paxton's structure, described by Thackeray as a 'blazing arch of lucid glass', and subsequently dubbed the 'Crystal Palace' by the magazine *Punch*,[3] was so unlike anything seen before that it captivated the public. So innovative was the design that excursions were organised from all parts of the country to enable people to see for themselves Paxton's masterpiece. This resulted in healthy profits for both the railway companies and the organisers, both of whom were reluctant to contemplate the demolition of the structure when the Exhibition closed.

This was, however, inevitable since it had required an Act of Parliament to site the Crystal Palace in Hyde Park, and the Commissioners had given an undertaking to vacate the site and to remove the building within seven months after the close of the Exhibition. Consequently, although Joseph Paxton actively campaigned to keep the Crystal Palace in Hyde Park to be used as a Winter Garden,[4] it was eventually decided that the structure should be dismantled and re-erected in another location. However, the Government would not sanction the use of public money for this purpose, and it was eventually left to a private company to purchase the building for £70,000 and arrange for its removal.

Thus the Crystal Palace Company was floated with a capital of £500,000. In its prospectus the company stated that the purpose of the rebuilt Palace would be to provide '... refined recreation, calculated to elevate the intellect, instruct the mind, improve the hearts of, and welcome the millions who have now no other incentives to pleasure but such as the gin-palace, the dancing saloon and the ale house afford them.' [5]

However, the Chairman of the company, Samuel Laing, and a co-director, Leo Schuster, were also respectively Chairman and co-director of the London, Brighton & South Coast Railway. Both men were well aware of the fact that the Great Northern Railway Company had made considerable profit from the Great Exhibition, and this must have played a major part in the eventual decision to transfer the Crystal Palace to an elevated site in rural Sydenham, which was conveniently situated near to the London, Brighton & South Coast railway line. In this new location the rebuilt Palace could not fail to boost the profits of the London and Brighton company.

Leo Schuster owned Penge Place, a large country mansion set in two hundred acres which was situated high up on the Sydenham ridge, less than a mile from the London, Brighton and South Coast main line. It was a prime location, with magnificent views of rural Kent and Surrey to the south, whilst to the east, London and the River Thames could be seen. Samuel Laing, anticipating that it would be relatively easy for the railway company to construct a short branch line to bring passengers to this site, persuaded Schuster to sell his property for £86,661 to the Crystal Palace Company to be used as the new location for the Crystal Palace.

However, the scheme met with strong opposition at an extraordinary meeting of the London, Brighton & South Coast Railway held at the Bridge House Hotel, Southwark, on the 4th June 1852, when Laing and Schuster were unable to convince those present that the arrangements with the Crystal Palace Company would be advantageous.

There was concern that railway profits might fall into the hands of the Crystal Palace Company, and it was therefore decided that a ballot should be held amongst the shareholders. This caused the proceedings to be delayed for a period of three weeks.

At a further extraordinary meeting held on 22nd June 1852, Laing, seconded by Schuster, put forward a second motion:

*

That the Directors be authorised to take the necessary steps for carrying into effect the general objects of the arrangements proposed to be entered into with the Crystal Palace Company.

*

However, many of the shareholders present were still extremely dissatisfied and Samuel Laing was presented with the following written protest:

*

We the undersigned shareholders in the London, Brighton and South Coast Railway do hereby protest against any agreement with the Crystal Palace Company whereby they shall participate in the income of the London, Brighton and South Coast Railway Company present or future or any part thereof. And generally against the proposed Agreement with the Crystal Palace Company.[6]

*

Despite this objection the motion was eventually passed, and plans were immediately put in hand to re-erect the Crystal Palace at Sydenham.

Plate 4 - Postcard view of Sydenham Hill, written on 26th March 1906 in a far more tranquil age. The Hill presented a fearsome 1 in 8 gradient against the horses as they transported the materials for the rebuilding of the Crystal Palace at its new site.

Author's collection

Plate 5 (Opposite) - The Brighton company's Low Level station, sometime between 1898 and 1905, when the overall roof was removed. Ultimately, George Moger was trading from both Crystal Palace stations as a coal merchant and one of his wagons is pictured here.

Neil Parkhouse collection

The Crystal Palace Company soon re-appointed Messrs Fox & Henderson as the contractor to re-erect the Palace and Charles Wild was again appointed as engineer in charge of the works. Paxton, who was also a director of the company, set about designing a new Crystal Palace and, following demolition of the Hyde Park structure, a start was made on transporting the building materials to Sydenham. This proved to be a laborious business as the materials had to be brought 20 miles by road by horse-drawn vehicles, and the horses had to negotiate a 1 in 8 gradient at Sydenham Hill to reach the Palace site. However, word of the project soon spread and navvies anxious to obtain work started to arrive from all parts of the country, until nearly 5,000 men were resident in the surrounding districts.[7]

At a ceremony held on the 5th August 1852 Samuel Laing erected the first column of the new Crystal Palace. Its construction was to continue for twenty months, involving the use of 9,641 tons of iron, 175 tons of bolts and rivets, 103 tons of nails and twice as much glass as had been used in the building in Hyde Park.[8] The resulting structure had three transepts, the main one being 200ft in height, and was 1,608ft in length, with a maximum width of 384ft. Inside it was divided into a series of palaces, Egyptian, Assyrian, Grecian, Byzantine, Moorish, German, French, English and Italian. These palaces, with the exception of the Egyptian, were set out on the scale of the originals, to enable the public to gain an insight into the architecture of different ages. Statues were prominent throughout the building, as were displays of works of art and rare shrubs and plants.[9] Paxton had also laid out grounds which were intended to rival those at Versailles, with fountains which required a supply of water at a rate of 120,000 gallons a minute. This was provided by water towers, designed by the celebrated Victorian engineer I. K. Brunel, which were to be situated at each end of the building.

The London, Brighton & South Coast Railway obtained parliamentary approval for its branch line on 8th July 1853, and work was soon in progress. Gangs of navvies could be seen excavating the cutting through Penge Woods, and in less than a year a curved line of just over one mile in length had been constructed which ran from Sydenham station to a terminus in the Palace grounds.[10] The station was situated at a level below that of the new Palace structure, and in order to accommodate this a covered walkway, 200 yards in length, was constructed to convey the passengers up into the new building. Construction work was completed on the 27th March 1854, when the new line was opened to freight traffic to enable materials to be transported to the Crystal Palace site.

The railway company had spent £85,000 on the construction of its branch line and station, and an impression of the elegance of the completed building can be gained from the following description given by Gordon Biddle in *Victorian Stations*:

*

Crystal Palace Low Level had a faintly French Renaissance frontage with unequal pavilion roofs and an elegant five-bay iron porte cochère. The usual Brighton lantern rose over the iron-ribbed booking hall roof, and, below, a low crescent-shaped twin-span roof formed the trainshed between heavily buttressed brick screen walls sporting blind acarding and massive end-blocks. Three 'grand staircases' with huge stone-capped newel posts and copings, ensured rapid entry and exit for the crowds.[11]

*

Anticipating that the Palace would attract many thousands of visitors, the company also arranged for a separate line of rails to be laid from London to its new station to accommodate only 'Crystal Traffic'.[12] Special locomotives were commissioned to haul these trains, as the gradient encountered from Sydenham station to the Crystal Palace was one of the most excessive on the London, Brighton and South Coast system.[13] The new service was extensively advertised in the press, prospective passengers being informed that '... special trains will run from London Bridge to the Crystal Palace every weekday morning, at very short intervals, commencing at a quarter of an hour before the hour of opening the Crystal Palace, and returning from the Crystal Palace in the evening, in a similar manner. The times of departure will be regulated by the hours at which the Palace is opened or closed.'[14]

Return fares, which included entrance to the Crystal Palace, were set as follows:

	First class	Second class	Third class
On shilling days	2s 6d	2s 0d	1s 6d
On half-crown days	4s 6d	4s 0d	3s 6d
On five shilling days	7s 0d	6s 6d	6s 0d

By the time of the formal opening of the Crystal Palace, numerous lodging houses had come into existence for those wishing to spend more time in the healthy environment of the Sydenham district. Two new hotels were also completed in the area by 1854 to cater for the visitors. The Royal Crystal Palace Hotel was situated at the top of Anerley Hill, within a hundred yards of the entrance to the Palace. Set in two acres of grounds, the step at the front door of this hotel was said to be on a level with the gilded cross on the top of St Paul's Cathedral, giving residents splendid views across the countryside to the River Thames. The hotel was frequented by the nobility in its early days, providing accommodation for such as Prince Albert, the Kaiser, and contentiously Queen Victoria, who is said to have allowed the royal crest to be erected over the hotel entrance. Joseph Paxton lived in the hotel temporarily during the construction of Rockhills, his future home set near to the Palace.

The other hotel built in the area was the Queens Hotel near Beulah Hill. A billiard room and tap room were provided within the hotel, whilst the proximity of the Crystal Palace allowed guests to frequent the magnificent grounds and attend the displays and musical entertainments. Although situated further from the Palace than the Royal Crystal Palace Hotel, the Queens Hotel also catered for an exclusive clientele. The Duke of Wellington, Florence Nightingale and Emperor Frederick of Germany were all at some time guests.[15]

On 10th June 1854 Queen Victoria, accompanied by many other dignitaries, officially opened the Crystal Palace in front of over 40,000 spectators. Prominent amongst those present was Samuel Laing who, as Chairman of the Crystal Palace Company, escorted Queen Victoria and the Royal party into the grand transept. Laing then delivered a lengthy opening address in which he pointed out that the object of the new building was to perpetuate the civilising influences initiated by the Great Exhibition, and that 'Private enterprise, appealed to in the interests of civilisation, supplied the funds.' The opening of the Crystal Palace at Sydenham was an outstanding success for the London, Brighton & South Coast Railway. The first special train left London Bridge at 10am on the day of the opening, initiating a half hour service of 22 trains a day each way, and thereafter an ordinary days traffic on the line was to be 10,000 passengers.[16] The glass structure was so prominent that it could be seen for many miles, and certainly from London Bridge station if the official guide to the London, Brighton & South Coast Railway is to be believed:

*

The traveller on the Brighton Railway may have caught a glimpse of the great transept soon after he got clear of the London Terminus, for rearing its sparkling vault on the summit of a considerable eminence, it forms a landmark to the whole surrounding countryside.[17]

*

So popular did the Crystal Palace become that when special events took place the railway company often had difficulty in finding enough carriages. However, John Ruskin, who was at that time resident in nearby Herne Hill, was not impressed with the building '... in the course of the 19th century, we suppose ourselves to have invented a new style of architecture, when we have magnified a conservatory!'[18]

Samuel Laing left the London, Brighton & South Coast Railway in 1855 to take up a government post in India, and in recognition of his work for the company an 0-4-2 locomotive No.199 carried the name *Samuel Laing* until it was withdrawn in 1925.[19] His place as Chairman was to be taken by Leo Schuster; however, this proved to be an unfortunate appointment in view of the fact that he nearly bankrupted the company. It is therefore perhaps not surprising that Schuster resigned in 1866, allowing Samuel Laing to return to the London, Brighton & South Coast Railway as Chairman in 1867.[20]

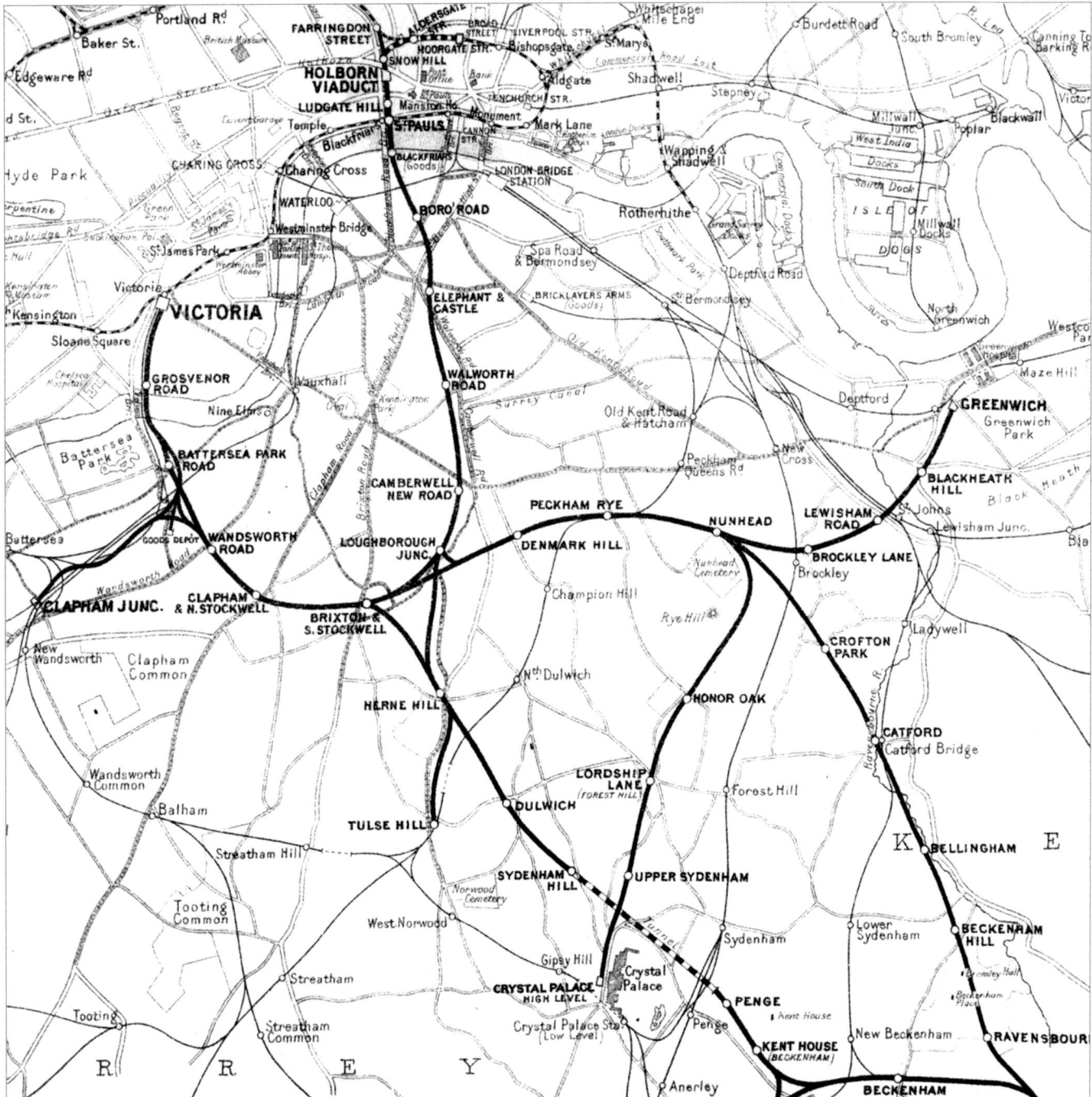

Figure 1 - This London, Chatham & Dover Railway map from an 1893 public timetable shows its lines in the London area *(in bold)* in relation to the lines of other companies. The London, Brighton & South Coast company had reaped the benefits from a substantial increase in traffic thanks to the removal of the Crystal Palace from Hyde Park, in London, to Sydenham and its opening on its new site in June 1854. This had not gone unnoticed by the London, Chatham & Dover Railway who considered that they, too, could attract some of the traffic from London that visited the Crystal Palace.

That company was a force behind the promotion of the Crystal Palace & South London Junction Railway, essentially an extension of the LC&DR but promoted as a separate company, to make a junction at Nunhead and take a southerly route to a new High Level station at the Crystal Palace. When construction started the contractor, Peto & Betts, was already working on the tunnel between what became Sydenham Hill and Penge stations, so any problems with getting materials to the new workings were minimised.

Map courtesy Neil Sprinks

❀ *Chapter Two* ❀

THE BIRTH OF THE CRYSTAL PALACE & SOUTH LONDON JUNCTION RAILWAY

The opening of the new Crystal Palace soon had an effect upon the surrounding area of Sydenham. The population rose steadily as merchants and their families moved in and set up shops and small businesses to cater for the increasing number of visitors, and soon the Crystal Palace became the most popular venue in London. Thousands flocked to London Bridge station in order to reach Sydenham, and on one day alone in 1859, one hundred and twelve thousand people were conveyed to the Low Level station to visit the Crystal Palace.[1] In view of the healthy profit that this generated for the London, Brighton & South Coast Railway it is not surprising that the company was anxious to maintain a monopoly position. However, the success of the Crystal Palace was sufficiently well publicised to attract the attention of rival railway companies.

In 1856 the West End of London & Crystal Palace Railway opened a service to Wandsworth Common and by 1860 this line had been extended to reach Victoria. In order to accommodate this line the London, Brighton & South Coast Railway modified its station at Crystal Palace so that a 'west station' was created in addition to the 'east station' which served the Sydenham branch. When the line from the 'west station' was eventually linked to Bromley in the south via Norwood Junction, the London, Chatham & Dover Railway Company was given permission to run trains into London by this route on condition that it would not convey passengers to the Crystal Palace.[2] There is no doubt that this was a useful arrangement for the London, Chatham & Dover Railway Company, but the Crystal Palace traffic was obviously lucrative, and the company soon became closely involved in a scheme to construct an alternative railway line which would allow visitors to arrive at the Palace entrance without having to undergo the steep climb from Crystal Palace Low Level station. The scheme involved the construction of a line, 6¼ miles in length, which would run through Peckham, to a new terminus almost directly in front of the Palace building.[3] This line was to be owned by a company to be called the Crystal Palace & South London Junction Railway, but it would be worked by the London, Chatham & Dover Railway Company in return for an agreed share of the profits.

The Crystal Palace & South London Junction Railway Company faced a number of difficulties in bringing its scheme to fruition. Eighteen hundred yards of the new line was to run across land owned by Alleyn's College of God's Gift, and the railway company was therefore obliged to carry out detailed negotiations with the Estate Governors of this organisation in order to agree terms.

It was also apparent that the route chosen for the railway would present engineering difficulties, as it would involve the excavation of a long deep cutting through unstable ground, and would also necessitate the speedy construction of two tunnels to enable excavation work to proceed at the site of the terminal station. Even when complete the line would challenge the locomotives of the London, Chatham & Dover Railway, as the gradient was to be set at 1 in 68 for most of the way.

On the 4th January 1862 the Executive Committee of Alleyn's College of God's Gift met to discuss the route of the proposed Crystal Palace & South London Junction line across its land. It was noted that 13 acres would be required and that two bridges would need to be constructed, one over Lordship Lane and the other over nearby Cox's Walk. The Governors were made aware of the fact that the railway would not alter the levels of any public road or path, and that the work would not affect the appearance of their estate as it would nearly all be carried out in cutting or tunnel.[4] However, concern was expressed at the inconvenience likely to be suffered by College tenants on Sydenham Hill '... whose property can hardly fail to be much depreciated by the noise and vibration of the railway traffic passing close to their lower boundaries.'

The Governors must also have been aware of the engineering difficulties likely to be encountered in the woodland of the Sydenham ridge, since they resolved that '... the mode of formation of this railway must also be carefully watched, so far as regards the deep and possibly dangerous side cutting in the wood.'[5]

The Crystal Palace & South London Junction line was not the only project to be discussed at this meeting. The Governors had also been approached by the London, Brighton & South Coast Railway with an alternative proposal to construct a railway which would leave their main line near New Cross station, traverse Peckham Rye and Dulwich, and join the West End of London & Crystal Palace Railway at Gipsy Hill station. The Governors were not slow to realise that two competing schemes gave them an advantage in negotiations, a fact borne out by the minutes which state that '... it is hardly likely that both lines will be sanctioned by Parliament, and there can be no doubt that both companies will be anxious to buy off the College opposition, so that it would seem that the Governors can take a very independent view of the two schemes.'[6]

The Governors took no final decision about either scheme, the matters being referred to a special meeting to be held on the 9th January 1862. On the day before this, however, the Crystal Palace & South London Junction Railway Company held its first directors' meeting, at which Sir Charles Rich, who was also on the board of the London, Chatham and Dover Railway, was appointed as Chairman and Mr F. F. Turner was appointed as engineer. At the meeting it was resolved that '... a communication be addressed to the London Chatham & Dover Railway Company offering to proceed to Parliament for the line and to make an arrangement with that company to work it upon terms to be agreed upon provided the London Chatham & Dover Railway Company will pay the expenses of the application to Parliament in case of failure.' [7]

The next day the Governors of Alleyns College of God's Gift met to discuss the two railway proposals. It was revealed that further discussions had taken place with one of the companies involved and '... that in the course thereof they had been urged by promoters of the Crystal Palace & South London Junction Railway, which is amalgamated with the London, Chatham & Dover Railway, to oppose the London & Brighton Bill on standing orders, in consequence of some insufficiencies of Notices which could only be objected to by the College.'

The Governors had already expressed some misgivings about the London, Brighton & South Coast Railway scheme. The damage caused to the estate would undoubtedly be very great and there seemed to be no compensatory benefit, except for the possibility of a station to serve Dulwich which would be located at Lordship Lane. It was therefore resolved to arrange '... a proper Bargain and Agreement with the London Chatham & Dover Railway Company', and all the Governors present then signed a memorial in opposition to the Brighton company.[8] This agreement enabled the College Governors to raise £26,500 from the sale of land which would subsequently be used to form part of the Crystal Palace Parade and to build the new the Crystal Palace station.[9] A further £13,500 was raised by selling land for the construction of the railway line from Herne Hill to Penge, and the money obtained from both sales was eventually used to build Dulwich College in College Road.[10]

The Crystal Palace & South London Junction Railway Company was also successful in concluding an agreement with the London, Chatham & Dover Railway Company on the future working of the line, and in June 1862 the terms of this agreement were set out as follows:

*

That the Crystal Palace & South London Junction Railway complete the line with stations, telegraphs etc and maintain it for twelve months to the satisfaction of the London Chatham & Dover Railway. The London Chatham & Dover Railway to work the line from the date of completion paying rates and all other charges except those of direction and office and to maintain the way and works after 12 months. The receipts from traffic booked from any station on the Metropolitan Extension lines of the London Chatham & Dover Railway to stations on the Crystal Palace line and vice versa and the receipts from traffic earned locally upon the Crystal Palace line will form the gross receipts from which the working expenses of the London Chatham & Dover Railway will be deducted to the extent of not less than 50% and not more than 60%. The surplus receipts will be paid to the Crystal Palace line until they reach 4½% on the capital not to exceed £900,000 after which any excess will be divided in equal proportions between the companies.[11]

*

Meanwhile Frederick Turner, the Engineer of the Crystal Palace & South London Junction Railway, faced questions from a House of Commons Committee about the proposed gradients of the new line. Turner was an experienced civil engineer who by 1862 had acquired a considerable knowledge of railway construction. He had previously been responsible for surveying and drawing up plans for lines in Sussex, Staffordshire and Shropshire, and had also been involved on railway works in Spain and Russia. From 1854 he was to be continuously employed on the development of the railway system in Kent, and it was said of him that:

*

Having once walked through a district and sketched out the route, it was seldom that any alteration was found necessary when the sections were taken.[12]

*

He was obviously able to assure the House of Commons Committee as to the feasibility of the High Level line to the Crystal Palace, for on the 17th July 1862 an Act authorising the railway was passed. The Crystal Palace & South London Junction Railway Company then instructed its solicitors, Messrs Freshfields & Newman, to begin purchasing land so that construction work could begin.[13] This work continued into 1863, and by August eighty-three notices had been served, and thirty purchases effected '... including the interest of some of the largest and most important owners, viz the Governors of Alleyn's College, Dulwich and their lessees, and the Directors of the Crystal Palace Company and their lessees ...' [14]

The importance that the Crystal Palace Company attached to the project can be gauged from the following report made by the directors to a shareholders' meeting in 1862:

*

The intended metropolitan extension of the London Chatham & Dover Railway, under the name of the Crystal Palace & South London Junction, the bill for which has very recently passed, cannot fail to be of material importance to this company. This line will leave the main line of railway at Camberwell Green, and will pass from thence by Peckham and Forest Hill to the Palace. It will thus have the advantage of two metropolitan termini, viz Victoria and Fleet Street, and will afford access to very large and populous suburban districts on the South of London which have hitherto been without direct communication, and as it will have the additional advantage of landing the passengers almost on the level of the floor of the Palace, a large increase in the number of visitors from town may also be looked for by this route. The station will be in the Dulwich wood, close to the road in front of the Palace, from which a direct access will be obtained below the road into the building. The directors have concluded an arrangement with the railway company for the land in Dulwich wood, by which the interests of the proprietors in this company are amply and advantageously protected.[15]

*

When an initial list of shareholders was drawn up on the 30th December 1862, there could be no doubt that the Crystal Palace & South London Junction Railway Company was closely connected to the London, Chatham & Dover Railway. The list showed that nine people had subscribed a total of £675,000 to form the company, and that over half of this sum had been put forward by Samuel Morton Peto (£179,000) and Edward Betts (£162,000).[16] Peto had made a fortune from the construction of buildings such as the Lyceum, the Houses of Parliament, Nelson's Column and from overseas construction contracts. In 1846 he formed a partnership with his brother-in-law Edward Betts and together they were involved in the promotion and construction of numerous railways. The firm of Peto & Betts was almost exclusively utilised by the London, Chatham & Dover Railway Company for the construction of its lines, and it was the practice of the firm to fund many of the London, Chatham & Dover proposals and to undertake the contracts in return for London, Chatham & Dover shares.[17] Peto & Betts therefore practically owned the railway company, and nobody was surprised when they were given the contract to construct the Crystal Palace & South London Junction line.

CONSTRUCTION WORK COMMENCES

In 1861 the section of the London, Chatham & Dover line between Herne Hill and Beckenham, which included the low level Sydenham tunnel, was in progress, with Peto & Betts as main contractor for the works.[18] It was therefore relatively easy for Peto & Betts to supply labour for the High Level railway contract, as the firm was in the fortunate position of having most of its navvies temporarily quartered in nearby Sydenham, where accommodation was consequently at a premium. The navvies had to live near to their work and some of the residents at that time found it profitable to run boarding houses for these men. Many of the bedrooms of these houses were continuously occupied, men from the night shift taking the beds vacated in the morning by men on the day shifts.

However, the men were apparently not hard to please, and were on the whole well behaved. Money changed hands pretty freely amongst them as long as it was available, and a number of local skittle alleys did good business, one of the most popular being a public house called The Beehive which was located in Wells Road.[19]

The contractor's Engineer and Agent in Sydenham was John Baldwin, who had first joined Peto & Betts in 1848 as Assistant Engineer and Agent for the construction of the Oxford & Birmingham Railway. Baldwin was so successful that Peto & Betts entrusted him with several other railway projects, and eventually he was placed in charge of the construction of the Sydenham low level tunnel. Engineering difficulties were soon encountered, as the ovoid section initially adopted for the tunnel lining proved unsuitable in London Clay and caused the tunnel to partially collapse. The dangerous nature of the work is illustrated by the following extract from Baldwin's diary:

*

April 5th, 1862 - Called up at 4.30am, the length next to the one now building at No.3 shaft having given way. I went down and through the debris into the inner length, and found the men had run out in great fear, as they had left their shirts, etc. I came back and went in again with foreman carpenter, and the length again made a start and dropped very near to my back, but I jumped into the inner length and escaped.[20]

*

Baldwin eventually overcame the difficulties by adopting

a circular section for the tunnel, but before the work was completed he was also given responsibility for the construction of the Crystal Palace & South London Junction Railway which commenced in 1863. This line would again involve extensive tunnelling, but fortunately Baldwin had already organised four large brickyards for the Sydenham works which were to eventually produce some fifty-five million bricks over a period of 2½ years.[21]

He soon deployed gangs of navvies at strategic points along the High Level line to begin the work of excavating the cuttings and forming embankments. A start was also made on the construction of the Crescent Wood tunnel, such that by August 1863 Frederick Turner was able to present the following report to the Directors of the Crystal Palace & South London Junction Railway Company '... the Contractors are carrying them (the heaviest works) forward with vigour at all available points by means of headings and shafts and in the Crescent Wood tunnel they have completed several lengths of the permanent work. The cuttings and embankments along the whole lengths for which land has been obtained are in full operation and are making rapid progress. The bridge over Lordship Lane and all other masonry in the foundation of the earthworks is in course of construction.' [22]

Work at the site of the new High Level terminus station had also progressed well. This was to be situated on a platform cut into the hillside at a level below that of Crystal Palace Parade, and consequently a long retaining wall had to be built to prevent any subsidence.[23] The excavated soil could not, however, be removed and had to be stored on site to await the completion of the tunnels. By November 1863 so much soil had accumulated on the site that Peto and Betts submitted a request to the College Governors for the use of a nearby field. This was granted on the condition that the contractor should be charged, and that '... the top surface of any deposit should not exceed the level of the crown of the road, and that the lower edge of the deposit against the road level be gently sloped off.'

This was one of many stipulations to be made by the Governors. They also insisted on the removal of all earth taken from working shafts '... under a penalty of £20 a day for non-removal after due notice given', and they reserved the right to decide upon the style and materials to be used in the construction of the station at Lordship Lane and the nearby Lordship Lane road bridge.[24]

It was not until early in 1864 that Peto & Betts were in possession of all the land necessary for the construction of the railway, the stations and their approaches. By that time one third of the total excavation of the cuttings had been completed, and both the 400yd Crescent Wood and 439yd Paxton tunnels were half finished. Turner was confident that the line would be completed by the Spring of 1865,[25] but it was already becoming apparent that the completion of the stations would be problematic.

In January the College Governors reported that '... a Memorial having been received from the College tenants at Sydenham Rise and other occupants of adjacent lands (not College tenants) praying the Governors to use their influence to induce the Crystal Palace & South London Junction Railway

Company to place their intended Lordship Lane station on the north side of that road, instead of in the position indicated in the College Agreement with the company on the south side, the Clerk do send to the Memorialists a copy of the Engineer's letter on the subject showing the impossibility of acceding to their request.' [26]

Having refused to change the location, it was then found that there was insufficient space for the construction of the approach to Lordship Lane station, and it therefore became necessary to make further application to the Governors in order to purchase additional land. Money problems were already beginning to beset the railway company, for in addition to the expense involved in purchasing the land and carrying out building work to the standard demanded by the College Governors, the company had commissioned Edward Barry to design a terminus at Crystal Palace which would cost around £100,000. In June 1864 the directors took the decision '... that the Board cannot sanction any expenditure on stations beyond the amount already settled, as the amount appears fully sufficient to give the accommodation required for the efficient working of the traffic.'

However, only two months later, when the financial situation had further deteriorated, the directors resolved that '... no permanent station except that for the Crystal Palace be erected at present.' [27]

After the 1862 Act authorising the Crystal Palace & South London Junction Railway had been passed, the London, Chatham & Dover Railway Company reached agreement with the London, Brighton & South Coast Railway over the shared use of lines to the Crystal Palace. Under the terms of the agreement, the London, Chatham & Dover Railway would be allowed to run over the Brighton company's lines between Peckham Rye and Brixton, whilst in return the London, Brighton & South Coast Railway would be allowed use of the Chatham company's lines between Brixton and Battersea for its proposed South London Railway.[28] It was during the construction of the lines at Brixton that a major accident occurred. Between 9 and 10pm on Friday, 12th February 1864, no fewer than nineteen arches of the South London Railway, which were in the course of construction, fell to the ground. These arches were unusually tall but were said to be solidly built using the best bricks. They had only been finished about ten days previously; however, despite a sudden change in weather from frost to rain, the shoring under them had been removed. This was considered to be the primary cause of the accident. Fortunately no lives were lost as there were no workmen on the site at the time.[29]

The Crystal Palace & South London Junction Railway Company held its fourth half yearly shareholders' meeting in September 1864, at which the directors were able to report that the brickwork in the Paxton and Crescent Wood tunnels was almost finished, and that '... the viaduct at Peckham, the bridges over the public roads, the works for the accommodation of the landowners, and the culverts under the embankments, are either complete or in course of construction.'

Over 180,000 cubic yards of material had already been excavated at the site of the Crystal Palace station and only 7,000 cubic yards remained. The Chairman reported that the contractor was awaiting the completion of the tunnels so that some of the soil could be used to finish the first portion of the long embankment near to Nunhead. He also pointed out that the total earth works for the line, from Peckham to the Crystal Palace, was estimated at 411,000 cubic yards and that so far 241,000 yards had been moved. Expenditure for the half year was given as £241,537, an average of approximately £9,000 per week.[30] (The embankment at Nunhead was part of a spur which had been authorised earlier in the year to connect the Crystal Palace and Greenwich branches, both of which were then under construction. The spur was partly constructed but never completed, and eventually an Act for its abandonment was obtained on 16th July 1874.) [31]

Two months later the Crescent Wood tunnel was completed, and the *Croydon Times* gave the following account of the ceremony which was held in order to record the laying of the last brick:

*

On Saturday the 12th November an interesting ceremony took place in the Crescent Wood tunnel, on the South London and Crystal Palace Railway, which was to place in position the last brick of the tunnel at the entrance in Wells Road, Upper Sydenham. The inside of the entrance was tastefully fitted up with evergreens. A champagne luncheon was provided in the most excellent style by Mr Collins of the Longton Grove Hotel. About two o'clock the company, consisting of about thirty ladies and gentlemen arrived. Amongst them were - Mrs Baldwin, Misses Turner, Miss Roney, Misses Watson, Mr Turner (principal engineer of the line), Mr Shelford, Mr Crampton, Mr Watson, Mr Baldwin, Mr Thorn, and Mr Hart. All the preliminary arrangements having been made the party ascended the scaffold, and the brick having been properly cemented by Mr Willis one of the sub-contractors it was placed in the hands of Miss Roney, who cleverly fixed it amidst loud cheers. Miss Roney then announced that the last brick of the Crescent Wood tunnel was placed in its final position; and gave a handsome donation for distribution amongst the workmen present.[32]

*

Work on the Paxton tunnel was to continue for a further three months, until in February 1865 Turner was able to report that it was finished and that the excavation of all of the cuttings was complete. He also noted that the viaduct at Peckham, and all of the bridges along the line, were nearing completion and that the contractor had commenced ballasting and laying the permanent way.[33]

Work on the newly named 'Crystal Palace and Upper Norwood' terminus was also well advanced. This was an elaborate structure designed to match the grandeur of the Crystal Palace itself. Built by a sub-contractor, Messrs Lucas, it is described by Gordon Biddle in *Victorian Stations* as follows '... an amazing structure, each corner occupied by a broad square tower with four French turrets apiece like miniature castles. Blind arcading with glazed upper sections appeared in the long side screen walls, and end walls were provided as well, with four square openings to admit the trains ... Platforms

Plate 6 - Taken from a painting of 1865 showing the exterior of Crystal Palace High Level station. The train shown leaving the station would appear to be hauled by one of the two engines which the London, Chatham & Dover Railway Company purchased from Hawthorn in 1860. These 2-2-2 engines proved to be unsuccessful and were replaced by 0-4-2 tank locomotives.

Reproduced by kind permission of the Governors of Dulwich College

were built on both sides of the centre tracks to ensure rapid alighting and boarding, and two circulating areas were built on bridges above them. The whole was enclosed by a two-bay roof, crescent-shaped like the Low Level station, on a central brick arcade. Heavy rustication, banded brick and tile work and an elaborate parapet completed the external adornment of this, the Chatham's most extravagant station.' [34]

The September 1865 issue of the *Illustrated London News* was also enthusiastic about the new Crystal Palace station, and in particular about the facilities afforded to 1st class passengers:

*

The High Level Crystal Palace Station

...the superior convenience of the new Crystal Palace station is already felt by many visitors who take their passage either from Victoria or Ludgate Hill stations of the London Chatham & Dover Railway Company in order to avoid the tedious walk up half a mile of corridors and staircases imposed on those arriving by the Brighton Company's line ... The platform of the station being on a level with the lower floor in the machinery department of the Crystal Palace, the passengers will have easy access by a handsome and well lighted subway 40ft wide, ascending to the main floor either in the centre transept or behind the concert room, by a broad flight of steps ... the distance from the station to the central transept is only 30 yards ... The station has four platforms, of which two are set apart for the use of 1st class passengers only ... all

the arrangements for 2nd and 3rd class passengers being distinct from those for 1st class passengers ...There will be room in the station and sidings for engines and carriages enough to carry away 7000 or 8000 passengers in an hour, and there is ample accommodation for goods traffic. [35]

*

The High Level line was officially opened on the 1st August 1865, although the August 1865 report submitted by Frederick Turner to the Crystal Palace & South London Junction Railway Company states that 'The works were completed, and the line opened for traffic on the 1st July last.' [36] The opening of the line allowed trains to run direct from Crystal Palace to Victoria, although there were no intermediate stations, and the terminus was only partially operational. Fortunately work on the intermediate stations progressed rapidly and on 1st September 1865 Lordship Lane was opened, followed by another three stations on the 1st December, Honor Oak on the High Level line, and Peckham Rye and Denmark Hill on the South London line. [37]

The subway which was supposed to convey 1st class passengers from the new terminus directly into the Crystal Palace had also not been completed in time for the opening of the line. It was the intention of the Crystal Palace & South London Junction Railway Company that this subway should match the architectural splendour of the station, and the company therefore engaged Italian cathedral craftsmen to create a Byzantine style structure consisting of a series of octagonal columns supporting a vaulted ornamental red and

Plate 7 - This picture, taken from a postcard and reproduced in its proper colours on the book cover, is of Lordship Lane station, painted by Camille Pissarro in 1871. The view was originally thought to have been of Penge East station.   *Courtesy Courtauld Institute Gallery*

white brick roof.[38] Whilst in retrospect such lavish expenditure on the Crystal Palace and Upper Norwood terminus appears to be extremely foolhardy, at the time there was still considerable public optimism about the future locations likely to be served by the new station:

*

When all the authorised lines of the Chatham and Dover Railway are complete, the new station will communicate directly with the stations at Victoria, Farringdon Street, Charing Cross, Cannon Street, London Bridge, Kings Cross, Paddington, all stations on the Metropolitan and Great Northern Railways and with Clapham, Brixton, Camberwell, Deptford, New Cross, Greenwich, Woolwich, and all stations on the South Eastern Railway and London South Western Railways.[39]

*

The press and the public may have been enthusiastic, but the directors of the Crystal Palace & South London Junction Railway Company must have been extremely concerned about the future viability of the line. The company had committed a lot of money to the construction of what was so far only a branch railway. The directors were therefore anxious to extend the line beyond the Crystal Palace in order to ensure maximum usage, but all attempts to achieve this had so far ended in failure. It was apparent that the future of the line remained heavily dependent on the success of the Crystal Palace, and this success could obviously not be guaranteed indefinitely.

ABORTIVE NEGOTIATIONS

The Crystal Palace & South London Junction Railway Company never intended its Crystal Palace & Upper Norwood station to remain as a terminus. Incorporated in the Act of 17th July 1862, which authorised the railway, was a proposal to extend the High Level line to South Norwood, then east to the Beckenham area via Bromley Junction. As an alternative it was proposed to extend the line north west through Lower Norwood to Streatham Hill.[40] Neither of these lines was completed and the railway company therefore turned its attention to Croydon as an alternative source of passengers. In 1865 a Bill was submitted to Parliament which proposed the extension of the High Level line to Croydon, with intermediate stations to be located at Beulah Spa and Thornton Heath. The trains would return to the Crystal Palace via an additional station to be placed at Addiscombe. The scheme was immediately opposed by the London, Brighton & South Coast Railway which already operated a service to Croydon, and a select committee was therefore appointed to examine the evidence for and against the Bill.

On Monday, 27th April 1865, the committee met in the House of Commons and heard evidence in support of the proposed line from Mr Robert Bowley, manager of the Crystal Palace. Bowley stated that the project was supported by the Board of Directors and all of the shareholders. He pointed out that the line would result in a large increase in traffic, and that it would enable visitors from Croydon to visit the Crystal

Palace without having to arrive at the Low Level station of the Brighton company where they were then forced to climb over 200 steps in order to enter the building. He drew attention to the popularity of the Crystal Palace, giving as an example the fact that whereas in one year 1,681,249 people visited Windsor Castle, the Houses of Parliament, Hampton Court, the British Museum, the National Gallery, the Tower of London and Kew Gardens, 1,681,083 visited the Palace in the same period. The new station at Beulah Spa would, he suggested, also attract passengers as it was one of the most attractive and beautiful spots in the neighbourhood of London, and a favourite resort during the summer months for persons who visited the long range of hills from Forest Hill beyond Beulah Spa for health purposes.

When Mr William Drummond, solicitor of Croydon and a member of the Croydon Local Board of Health, was examined he also spoke enthusiastically about the proposed line. He said that the people of Croydon were at the mercy of the Brighton and South Eastern Railways, and in support of this he produced a copy of the following agreement between the two companies:

*

There shall not at any time hereafter be between the two companies any competition in the way of fares or rates for traffic between London and Croydon, including Addiscombe; but for all traffic between London and Addiscombe, the South Eastern Company will adopt as their minimum fares and rates, the lowest fares and rates from time to time charged by the Brighton Company for traffic of like kind between London and any of the Brighton Company's stations at Croydon.

*

Mr Drummond was of the opinion that the people of Croydon would prefer to have a third company intervening, to break up the monopoly between the Brighton and the South Eastern. This view was supported by a number of local business men, who when called also spoke in favour of the line. It would, they said, boost the trade of the town generally, and would develop districts which had not yet been developed. It would also increase the value of houses already built.

On the second day of the hearing Mr Seymour Clarke, manager of the Great Northern Railway, was the first witness examined. He spoke of the advantages which the Great Northern Railway would gain by its connection via Smithfield with a High Level line serving the Crystal Palace and Croydon. The committee was informed that:

*

The Great Northern would, in the event of the Brighton or South Eastern declining to work the line, be prepared to work it, as they would then be enabled to take coals from the pit's mouth in the north, to Croydon, without breaking bulk. Croydon would then have the benefit of competition in coal. The Great Northern already had running powers over the London & Chatham line to work their trains from King's Cross, Ludgate, and Forest Hill, to the high level Crystal Palace; and it would be convenient for the Great Northern thence to work round by Croydon; and so back by Addiscombe back to London.

*

This testimony was then followed by that of Sir Samuel Morton Peto, of the firm Peto & Betts, who stated that his firm were prepared to undertake the works, including the purchase of land, for the sum of £400,000. Two civil engineers who had been involved in the survey and design of the proposed line were then called and questioned as to its feasibility. They both

Plate 8 - Iona Class 0-4-2T *Spey* built by Neilson & Co. of Glasgow in 1866. In 1878 this engine and ten suburban carriages were fitted with Smith's vacuum brake and trials were conducted between Victoria and Crystal Palace High Level.　　*National Railway Museum/SSPL*

Plate 9 - A damaged and quite poor photograph but included because it shows the High Level station at Crystal Palace when operated by the LC&DR in the 1890s and the earlier Saxby & Farmer signal box. Its date of replacement by a later and more conventional style Saxby & Farmer box is not known.   *Roger Carpenter*

confirmed that the construction of the railway would cause minimal disruption, and that it would be a valuable addition to the lines already operational in the area.

At this point in the proceedings the Crystal Palace & South London Junction Railway Company must have been confident that approval to extend the High Level line would eventually be obtained. However, the next witness, Mr John George Tollmache Sinclair of The Mount, lying between the Crystal Palace and Beulah Spa, spoke against the Bill as it would, he said, have a detrimental effect upon his property. He was followed by three other property owners who also gave the same reason for objecting to the proposed railway.

On the third day of the hearing the London, Brighton & South Coast Railway was allowed to voice its opposition to the Bill. Mr George Hawkins, the traffic manager of the company, emphasised the dangerous nature of the line. From the Crystal Palace it would be constructed at a gradient of between 1 in 70 and 1 in 80. It would not, he said, be safe or practicable to erect a station on any part of a line with such a gradient. He also pointed out that nine stations were either erected, or in the course of erection, in Croydon. The Brighton company had wharfs at Deptford and Battersea, both with direct railway access to Croydon; and they also had a connection with the Commercial Docks. In view of this he could not see any necessity for the new line, either for goods traffic or for local purposes. A further five witnesses were called by the Brighton company during the course of the day, and each stated that the new line would damage business interests in the Croydon area.

On the last day of the hearing the Secretary of the LB&SCR, Mr Slight, was the final witness who spoke against the Bill. The Committee then met in private, and after a short deliberation decided that a case for an extended High Level line had not been proved and the Bill was consequently thrown out.[41]

The lucrative traffic which would have resulted from the proposed extension of the High Level railway was thus denied to the Crystal Palace & South London Junction Railway Company. The situation was made worse by the fact that the London, Chatham & Dover Railway Company had failed to construct spurs which had been promised at Camberwell and Loughborough Junction. This not only reduced the likelihood

of companies such as the South Eastern being able to run trains to the Crystal Palace, it also left the Crystal Palace & South London Junction Railway Company with only indirect access to the City.[42] However, the idea of extending the High Level line was never to be forgotten and attempts to extend the line were to continue throughout the nineteenth century. In 1883 the London, Chatham & Dover Railway Company put forward another scheme to extend the line to Croydon, where it was to connect with the Oxted & Groombridge Railway.[43] This proved to be unsuccessful, so the following year an independent company sought to construct a railway '... from the Crystal Palace High Level station to a junction with the London Chatham & Dover Railway Company at Beckenham, with a branchline to connect it with the South Eastern Railway by a junction with that company's lines near Elmers End station.' [44]

A survey was carried out in December 1884 but it is likely that this related to yet another proposal to extend the line to West Croydon. However, by 1884 the area surrounding the High Level station had been developed, and local residents were concerned that railway construction work would damage their environment. The following letter to a local newspaper typifies the opposition to the proposal:

*

Sir,
Allow me to call your attention to a projected line of railway which threatens to invade our neighbourhood and disturb our repose. Mysterious looking individuals, armed with staves and levelling instruments, have been observed of late taking observations and notes, and when questioned state their mission to be an open cutting from the High Level station opposite the Crystal Palace, under or over the Tudor Road, and across Fox Lane to a point in the Sylvan Road, and thence to - Heavens knows where, destroying houses, gardens, meadows, and privacy en route! Any and every information you can gather and furnish on this subject will be of great interest to many of your readers, who forewarned may be forearmed.[45]

AN OLD RESIDENT.

*

Despite such objections, the proposed extension to West Croydon was still being considered in 1890 when the surveyor wrote to the *Sydenham & Penge Gazette* assuring its readers that '... the scheme will not affect any part of this district, although it is very close to the boundary of the parish of St Mary, Lambeth...'

No further reports appeared in the press, and the scheme was finally abandoned.[46]

THE EARLY YEARS

The week before the High Level line was officially opened it was inspected by Colonel Rich of the Railway Inspectorate. He found the new line to be satisfactory, and soon 19 trains were running on weekdays between Crystal Palace and Victoria. The opening was welcomed by the *South London Press* in an article which noted that the line served stations at Battersea Park, Stewarts Lane, Wandsworth Road, Clapham, North Stockwell and Brixton, and that:

*

Ultimately it is intended that there should be stations between Brixton and the Palace. At present the line is very little appreciated through its not being sufficiently known but ultimately, no doubt, the traffic will be very considerable.[47]

*

The Crystal Palace & South London Junction Railway Company held its half-yearly meeting on 23rd August 1865, and the Chairman was able to report that despite the fact that several stations were still in the course of construction, traffic on the line had increased daily. In the first week the trains carried between 4,000 and 5,000 passengers, in the second week this increased to 10,000, and in the third week to 20,000. The Chairman was therefore confident that the new line would prove to be a paying and profitable undertaking.[48] By 1866 there were 33 trains a day, the 9¼ mile journey to Victoria taking 40 minutes.[49]

However, the directors of the Crystal Palace & South London Junction Railway were still agitated by the failure of the London, Chatham & Dover Railway Company to provide them with a direct access to the City, and the minutes of a Board meeting held on the 28th February 1866 record that '... the line was originally projected to accommodate only the traffic of the London, Chatham & Dover Railway Company but during its construction very important arrangements have been made by which traffic from the South Eastern, the Great Northern, the Metropolitan, and probably the South Western, Railways will also be brought over it.'[50]

The initial level of traffic on the High Level line was encouraging, but the working agreement between the two railway companies soon ran into difficulty. The Chatham company, which was already in a precarious financial position when it began to operate the line, had gained a reputation for being inefficient and for providing old and dirty carriages for its trains.[51] The general public referred to the company as the 'Smash 'Em and Turnover', whilst travellers bemoaned the fact that 60% of London, Chatham & Dover trains failed to arrive on time. The shortcomings of the London, Chatham & Dover Railway Company were even raised in Parliament:

*

Its trains are formed of unclean cattle trucks propelled at snail-like speeds, with frequent stops of great length by Machiavellian locomotives of monstrous antiquity, held together by wire and rusty bolts. These locomotives groan, hiss, and ooze a scalding conglomeration of oil and water from every pore.[52]

*

One of these ancient locomotives is depicted in a painting, dated 1865, which is currently owned by Dulwich College. It is shown leaving the High Level station at Crystal Palace hauling a Chatham carriage typical of the period, and would appear to be one of the two engines which the London, Chatham & Dover Railway Company purchased from Hawthorn in 1860. These 2-2-2 locomotives had 5ft 9in driving wheels and were built without a protective cab for the driver. They were not successful engines and were soon replaced by 0-4-2T locomotives as the main source of power on the High Level line.[53]

❧

Plate 10 - London, Chatham & Dover Railway A1 Class 0-4-4T, possibly No.171, at Nunhead carrying the Crystal Palace headcode on 8th July 1899.

Ashford Local Studies Library

Plate 11 - The exposure fault at the left hand edge does little to detract from the elegance of the railway bridge at the approach to Lordship Lane station. The design, rather than being utilitarian, was in response to the requirements of the Governors of the Dulwich College Estate.

John Stanton collection

Elderly engines and cramped, dirty and badly furnished carriages were unlikely to be appreciated by the predominantly middle-class passengers that the Crystal Palace & South London Junction Railway Company were dependent upon. However, there was no possibility of any improvement in the situation, for in the Spring of 1866 the London, Chatham & Dover Railway Company was placed into receivership.

The event which precipitated the bankruptcy of the railway company was the collapse of certain banks in May 1866, which in turn led to the collapse of the firm of Peto & Betts. It has already been noted that this contractor regularly carried out construction work in return for shares in the Chatham company, and on the strength of the shares issued loans were then obtained through the issue of debentures. On the 30th June 1866 some of these debentures fell due, but because the firm of Peto & Betts had already gone into liquidation, the London, Chatham & Dover Railway Company became liable for a debt for which funds were not available. When the circumstances of the bankruptcy became known it was apparent that the London, Chatham & Dover Railway Company had been run for the benefit of the contractor, rather than for the shareholders.[54]

The High Level railway was now owned and operated by two penniless companies and the working of the line suffered accordingly. When the London, Chatham & Dover Railway Company complained that the signalling equipment and goods

facilities at the Crystal Palace terminus were inadequate, and that a carriage dock was required for the unloading of private carriages, the Crystal Palace & South London Junction Railway Company refused to take any action because of the lack of funds. This gave the Chatham company an excuse to withhold the payments which were due in accordance with the agreed working arrangements on the grounds that the line was unfinished. The Chatham company also refused to accept responsibility for any accidents resulting from the lack of proper signals, a decision which marked the beginning of a lengthy dispute between the two companies.[55]

The refusal to provide proper facilities for goods traffic was extremely short-sighted. There was a market for the distribution of goods and coal throughout the area served by the High Level line, and this should have provided the London, Chatham & Dover Railway Company with an additional source of income. However, the dispute with the Crystal Palace & South London Junction Railway Company prevented the speedy introduction of both goods and coal trains, and it was not until the early 1870s that the coal and goods facilities of the Crystal Palace terminus were fully operational. The firm of G. J. Cockerell & Co., which was initially unsuccessful in its attempt to rent part of the coal yard in 1868,[56] eventually established a successful business at the station yard which was advertised extensively in the local press:

∗
COALS

G. J. Cockerell & Co. of 13, Cornhill, Coal Merchants to Her Majesty and to the Royal Family, are supplying the inhabitants of Norwood, Sydenham, and the neighbourhood, with the best Wallsend Coals, or the best inland, brought to G. J. Cockerell & Co.'s Wharves at the High Level station, direct from the pits, in first rate condition for size and quality, and delivered at their London prices. Best Wallsend, 36s; Best Inland, 34s; Coke, 26s - Local Office, South Transept, Crystal Palace [57]

∗

In June 1870 Messrs Cockerell & Co. wrote to the Civil Engineer of the London, Chatham & Dover Railway requesting a supply of tapped water. The cost of providing this was high, as the pipe had to be laid across the running track and the sidings, and it was therefore suggested that all of the coal merchants share the cost so that all could enjoy the facility. [58]

The development of passenger traffic on the line was more successful, as the number of travellers continued to increase. Crowds still flocked to the Crystal Palace, even after a serious fire destroyed the northern transept in 1866, and on Boxing Day record numbers of passengers travelled on the special London, Chatham & Dover trains between Victoria, Ludgate Hill and the Crystal Palace terminus. The 'roving correspondent' of the South London Press observed that 10,000 people attended the event, and described in detail the unpleasant travelling conditions on the return journey:

∗

There is nothing more to be seen, and only time to be wasted in staying longer, so I make for the High Level station, and after a good use of whatever finesse I am gifted with, procure a seat. This must have been a very valuable thing, for ere the train started we were actually stormed by a crowd of impatient beings, who crossed the rails and tumbled into the compartments through the windows, and insisted willy nilly in sharing what we had obtained with such care and trouble. Thus packed and assorted - first, second, and third class all in a lump - we proceeded on our way, being luckily relieved at the different stations of a little of our load, and after due stoppage and changing at Brixton, reached home. [59]

∗

The opening of intermediate stations on the South London line greatly increased the number of passengers travelling to the Crystal Palace, as they gave the populations of districts such as Camberwell and Peckham access to a new source of entertainment. [60] However, the stations on the High Level branch at Honor Oak and Lordship Lane were less frequently used, both being set in semi-rural locations. Honor Oak was an entirely wooden structure which was built on an embankment, with wooden shelters on the platforms. The station master occupied a detached house at ground level which overlooked a wooden booking office. Surprisingly the station also boasted a small coal yard off the up line, which presumably served the new villas located on Forest Hill. The only other source of traffic was the nearby Camberwell cemetery. [61]

Lordship Lane was more elaborate in its appearance, due to the conditions imposed by the Estates Governors. A series of gothic arches at ground level enabled passengers to enter a substantial brick station building, with Tudor style chimneys, which opened onto the down platform at first floor level. (The up platform was reached by means of a subway.) Both platforms were sheltered by canopies with fretted valances which were supported by decorative columns. As at Honor Oak, passenger traffic was provided by nearby villas situated in Lordship Lane and Wood Vale. [62]

It was expected that the opening of Lordship Lane station would have an effect upon the development of the surrounding area, and in 1869 the South London Press published the following article:

∗

Lordship Lane is assuming quite a fresh character. Hitherto it has consisted chiefly of detached mansions and villas, but the building mania has seized hold of the district, and I now notice a row of shops erected on the Friern Manor Farm, facing the lane, which, besides being a novelty in itself, will have this effect - it will give a sort of village aspect to the neighbourhood. The inhabitants will be able to draw their supplies from home, instead of having to procure them from Peckham, Dulwich, and elsewhere. This is only a beginning; but given a railway station, an inn, and a row of shops, and a little town may in these fast days be confidently looked for. Within a few years building operations of an extensive nature will be in progress hereabouts. [63]

∗

Despite this optimism the 'little town' failed to materialise, with the result that the number of passengers using Lordship Lane station did not significantly increase until 1901, when the nearby Horniman Park and Museum was opened to the public.

The passenger traffic on the line was in the main generated by the Crystal Palace and Upper Norwood terminus, which by the late 1860s had begun to attract an increasing number of season ticket holders and regular travellers whose business interests necessitated their daily attendance in London. This traffic was placed in jeopardy in 1868 when the London, Chatham & Dover Railway, in conjunction with the other local railway companies, introduced a substantial fares increase. This immediately resulted in a decrease in the number of shilling visitors to the Crystal Palace, whilst regular passengers were so angry that they formed a committee and threatened to take only third class tickets when compelled to travel. Some even suggested that an approach should be made to the General Omnibus Company, or any other company that would be prepared to initiate a service into London. [64] However, none of these protestations proved to be effective as the new fares were not withdrawn and regular travellers had little option but to pay up.

This was to be the first of many fares increases to be introduced on the High Level line. It was inappropriate because the London, Chatham & Dover Railway Company was still heavily dependent on the Crystal Palace for passengers, so that any reduction in the number of visitors caused the railway to

Plate 12 - The influence of the Estate Governors is apparent in this latter-day view of Lordship Lane station frontage. *Lens of Sutton Association*

lose income. The situation was aggravated by the fact that the Crystal Palace was always closed on Sundays, as the religious beliefs of the Victorian middle classes dictated that Sunday should be treated strictly as a day of rest, despite the fact that this was the only leisure day available to many people.

The Chatham company was therefore unable to run excursion trains to the Palace on Sundays, even though they would have undoubtedly proved popular. In fact any form of Sunday working on the railways was resented on religious grounds, and petitions against such practices were not unknown. The following extract is taken from a petition received by the South Eastern Railway Company following a Sunday accident on the nearby North Kent line in 1857:

*

The undersigned are aware of the arguments used to justify or palliate the running of trains on the Lord's day for the alleged recreation of the working classes, and the convenience of the public, but they feel that no company of professing Christians is justified, on any such ground, in holding out special inducements to the desecration of the Lord's day.[65]

*

Throughout the nineteenth century the limitation of Sunday working was to badly affect the profitability of both the Crystal Palace Company and the railways serving the Crystal Palace. An early campaigner was the 19th century philanthropist Catherine Marsh, who actively campaigned against Sunday working in an attempt to obtain better rights for railway navvies in the Norwood area. In *English Hearts and English Hands* she appealed directly to landowners:

*

If each proprietor of land through whose ground the railway passes, would not sell it without making a stipulation that the working man should have his seventh days' rest secured, he would bring down a blessing on both souls and bodies, and would find that the Lord of the Sabbath would repay him seven fold into his own bosom.

*

Even as late as 1899, when Sunday concerts were introduced at the Crystal Palace, the Rev. Henry Stevens, vicar of Holy Trinity, Sydenham, issued a public protest:

*

These concerts on Sundays make the Crystal Palace a rival and competitor in respect of places of worship in drawing the people away from public services on Sunday afternoons, as well as from Bible classes and Sunday schools.

*

He was also unhappy that 'These costly Crystal Palace concerts ... must draw people not merely from Norwood and Sydenham, but from places all along the lines which lead to the Palace ...' and pointed out that this would involve public servants such as ticket clerks, ticket collectors, porters, conductors and drivers having to work on the railways on a Sunday.[66]

The Sunday Observance Acts were passed in the years 1625, 1677 and 1780. However, it was not until 1932 that the Sunday Entertainments Act repealed or rendered ineffective much that was contained within these old Acts, concerning cinemas, concerts and similar entertainments, museums, picture galleries, zoos, botanical gardens, aquaria and lectures or debates.[67]

Plate 13 - The closed Crystal Palace High Level branch on the extreme left curves away from the junction at Nunhead. *Lens of Sutton Association*

❀ **Pictorial survey - Nunhead** ❀

Plate 14 - Nunhead signal box after 1954. The brick wall is the end of some flats, which were built after that year. *Lens of Sutton Association*

Plate 15 - Nunhead station was remodelled as a single island platform, opening as such on 3rd May 1925. Apparently work is being undertaken on the underbridges and cable trunking. According to the locomotive's headcode, Class C No.31508 is working a Hither Green goods. The Up starter is still a semaphore signal which, by the time of *Plate 17*, had been replaced by a colour light signal.   *Lens of Sutton Association*

Plate 16 - Rail overbridge at Nunhead station on Saturday, 18th September 1954.   *Mile Post 92½ Picture Library; A W V Mace*

Plate 17 - A murky day in south London and very quiet at ten past two in the afternoon. This is Nunhead Up platform in British Railways days, evidenced by the colour-light signal as the Up starter, but is later than *Plate 15* when the Up starter was a semaphore. The posters are advertising Weymouth and Bournemouth.   *Lens of Sutton Association*

Plate 18 - The print is not sharp enough to identify this 4-SUB unit climbing away from Nunhead with the 3.37pm Blackfriars-Crystal Palace (HL) on 17th September 1954 with a glimpse of Nunhead's coal yard on the right. Telegraph poles carrying railway communications is a sight long gone. The nearest wavy pole may be a photographic aberration but the others this side of the signal box appear straight.   *Denis Cullum*

Chapter Three

THE LONDON, CHATHAM & DOVER TAKES OVER

In September 1866 the directors of the Crystal Palace & South London Junction Railway Company were forced to report that the company was still awaiting receipt of 40% of the earnings of the High Level line from the London, Chatham & Dover Railway. It was also noted that there was still no direct access to the City because of the failure of Messrs Peto & Betts, and that consequently it took over one hour to travel from the Crystal Palace to Ludgate Hill. This prompted complaints from shareholders that the directors had failed in their duty by not obtaining a written guarantee from the London, Chatham & Dover Railway Company to construct a direct City link via Peckham and Walworth. It was also suggested that the shareholders might have a claim against Sir Morton Peto in view of the loss of interest which they had suffered as a result of the failure of his firm.[1]

The anger expressed by the shareholders obviously had an effect upon the board, for by the time that the next half yearly meeting of the Crystal Palace & South London Junction Railway Company was held a new chairman, Mr J. E. Levenson-Gower, was in place. He informed the shareholders that all of the former directors of the company had resigned because of other engagements and that a new board of directors had been appointed. Mr Levenson-Gower then dealt with the shareholders' complaints by pointing out that the new board had no desire to rush into an expensive litigation in order to obtain the revenue to which they were entitled. He believed that in view of the 'high character' of the London, Chatham & Dover board, its directors would eventually act fairly in the matter. 'The company is like a ship,' he explained, 'high and dry - the timbers are sound, the bottom untouched. All we have to do is to wait until the tide comes up and floats us. If we attempt by litigation to drag the ship off we will knock a hole in the bottom.'

On being appointed as chairman Mr Levenson-Gower had, he said, made a full inspection of the line with the company engineer, and found that the works had been well constructed. He was therefore able to assure the meeting that '... with a line, one end of which touches one of the most beautiful places in the kingdom, and at the other one of the greatest cities in the world, we cannot but be successful.'[2]

However, the new directors soon discovered that the London, Chatham & Dover Railway Company had not insured any of the stations on the High Level line, and it was therefore hastily decided that the terminus at Crystal Palace should be insured for the sum of £25,000, the Lordship Lane station for £5,500 and the Honor Oak station for £4,500.[3] This action was

fortuitous as a minor fire was to occur two years later at the High Level station, as it had now become known, due to the overheating of a flue. The fire was soon extinguished but an eight foot length of staircase was destroyed.[4] There was shortly to be a further accident at the station when the 8.26am train to Victoria was involved in a collision whilst being shunted, due to a misunderstanding between the driver and the pointsman. Nobody was injured but a horse-box being used to transport animals from a dog show at the Palace was smashed, and another was badly damaged.[5]

The refusal of the London, Chatham & Dover Railway Company to hand over a proportion of the operating profits of the High Level line placed the Crystal Palace & South London Junction Railway Company in serious financial difficulty. The company was therefore unable to complete the purchase of some of the land near to Honor Oak station which had been used for the construction of the railway, and this resulted in two sales being held which were recorded as follows:

*

Sale No.1, in 1869, included two acres and 34 perches, being the whole of the rails, 933 feet in length, as well as the bridge at the Forest Hill Road crossing; while sale No.2, in 1871, comprised three acres, formerly part of Brockley farm, the property of the Earl of St. Germains, and extending about 1000 feet along the permanent way from the county and parish boundary northwards. It sold for £4000. Both sales took place through the Company failing to complete purchase.[6]

*

The subsequent arrangements made by the Crystal Palace & South London Junction Railway Company to continue using the High Level line are not recorded, but the sales may have been partly responsible for the company taking its dispute with the London, Chatham & Dover Railway Company to arbitration in 1869 in order to ease its financial problems. This tactic proved to be unsuccessful, for although two different arbitrators scrutinised the agreement between the two companies, each took a different view as to the meaning of the words 'Actual Cost of Working'. The arbitrators were therefore unable to determine the amount of money owing to the Crystal Palace & South London Junction Railway Company, much to the annoyance of its directors who complained that '... the Company is still liable to the cost, delay and annoyance of an arbitration every half year, with varying result ...'[7]

In 1870 the financial position of the London, Chatham & Dover Railway Company improved significantly when the company was discharged from bankruptcy as a result of a settlement engineered by the Lord Chancellor and the Marquis of Salisbury. The company no longer had to hire its rolling stock from creditors for the sum of £550 per week[8] and it was

(Left) Plate 19 - Full-page advertisement from a London, Chatham & Dover Railway public timetable of July 1893 highlighting the attractions and exhibitions at the Crystal Palace. *Courtesy Neil Sprinks*

Plate 20 - It is possibly 1897 and, although a very poor print, this is the only available view looking towards Upper Sydenham of Lordship Lane signal box, the siding connection of that period and, just round the bend, Cox's Walk footbridge.

John Stanton collection

also freed from the prospect of further litigation. Being in a much stronger position the company was now able to make improvements to the High Level line, and in September 1871 Crystal Palace trains were given access to a new station which was opened at Nunhead. This was followed in 1872 by the construction of a curve from Loughborough Junction station to a junction at Cambria Road on the Brixton to Peckham line. Although little more than a quarter mile in length, this curve reduced the journey between Ludgate Hill and the Crystal Palace by two miles, and eliminated the inconvenience of changing carriages at Brixton. The opening of this line was advantageous to residents living in the areas of Denmark Hill and Peckham Rye, and it also provided the London, Chatham & Dover Railway Company with an opportunity to increase passenger traffic by providing a more direct service to the City from the Crystal Palace.[9]

The loop line proved to be of immense benefit to the residents of Norwood and North Penge, resulting in an immediate increase in the number of passengers travelling between the High Level station and the City. The *Norwood News* seized the opportunity to campaign for a new entrance to be constructed at the High Level station for the benefit of the residents of nearby Farquhar Road. An editorial in the newspaper noted that the loop line now gave the London, Chatham & Dover Railway Company several advantages over its competitors, but pointed out that '... these inducements to patronage will be of very little avail unless the opening of the door at the south end of the High Level Station is conceded, and another entrance is made for those residing in the Farquhar Road. We doubt if any building of the immense size of the High Level Station has so absurdly few means of access or exit. ... the resident in the Farquhar Road beholds just outside his front window the train which he would have a very long trudge to reach, and is kept from the bosom of his family in some cases nearly half-an-hour longer per day than if the simple expedient of opening an entrance on his side of the station was adopted.'

The newspaper was also anxious to level a further complaint

against the London, Chatham & Dover Railway Company '... the Company have partly taken away with one hand what they gave with the other. Instead of all trains running direct to Victoria as heretofore, Crystal Palace passengers now not unfrequently have to change at Peckham Rye; the old Brixton sore thus breaking out in a fresh place. The loop line having been constructed to prevent the previous change, the step seems somewhat like falling upon Scylla while trying to avoid Charybdis.'[10]

There was certainly a need for better access to the High Level station for local residents but an additional entrance was not to be provided until 1876, when a footbridge was constructed from Farquhar Road into the first class area of the station.[11] At the same time a ticket office was opened at the Royal Crystal Palace Hotel, so that residents and others were able to obtain tickets for London without waiting at the High Level station booking office.[12]

The future of the High Level line seemed assured, for in addition to the increase in passengers travelling to the City, the Crystal Palace still drew enormous crowds. On Boxing Day 1872 a record number of visitors were recorded, and 15,000 of them were carried to the High Level station by London, Chatham & Dover trains. They travelled to view '... the beautiful scenery and spectacular effects of the Masque, the comic ballet of the Rowellas, the Herculean feats of the Beni-Zoug-Zoug Arabs, the brilliant Fancy Fair, and the lofty and gaily decorated Christmas Tree.'

Despite the fact that the High Level station was in constant use throughout the day, for the Palace was illuminated until 10pm, the event passed without any accident whatever.[13]

The changed circumstances of the London, Chatham & Dover Railway Company should have ensured an end to the dispute over the operating expenses on the High Level line. However, acrimony between the two companies was still continuing in 1874, and the reluctance of the London, Chatham & Dover Railway Company to compromise in this matter indicates that its directors had every intention of forcing the Crystal Palace & South London Junction Railway Company out of business.

At its half yearly meeting the directors of the Crystal Palace & South London Junction Railway Company reported that it was still not possible to reach agreement with the London, Chatham & Dover Company, and that consequently they were seeking links with other railway companies:

*

The Directors have deposited Bills in Parliament for making junctions with the South Eastern and London and Brighton Railways, and have received promises of support from both these Companies.[14]

*

Nothing was to come of the discussions which were subsequently held with the South Eastern and the London, Brighton & South Coast Companies, but the threat prompted the London, Chatham & Dover Railway Company to give its support to two schemes which were designed to damage the interests of the Crystal Palace & South London Junction Railway Company. The first proposal was to construct a new line which would give direct access to the Crystal Palace High Level station from Dulwich, whilst the second scheme involved the construction of a loop line from Beckenham which would give direct access to Crystal Palace Low Level station. The Beckenham loop line was actually constructed for the sum of £11,000,[15] but the proposed line from Dulwich, which would have posed considerable engineering difficulties, was eventually abandoned.

The financial position of the Crystal Palace & South London Junction Railway Company continued to worsen, and its directors were now forced to consider the prospect of amalgamation with the London, Chatham & Dover Railway Company as an alternative to further expensive litigation. By October 1874 a decision to proceed with the merger had been taken, and agreement was subsequently reached with the London, Chatham & Dover Railway Company on the 7th December 1874. The merger was approved at a final board meeting held on the 26th February 1875,[16] and on the 1st July 1875 the Crystal Palace & South London Junction Railway Company ceased to exist, when it was sold to the London, Chatham & Dover Railway Company under the terms of the London Chatham & Dover Act 1875.[17]

STAFFING THE RAILWAY

Although the railways offered secure employment, the 19th century railway worker faced long hours and low pay. Surviving records of the London & South Western Railway show that in 1843 enginemen were required to work an average week of fifty-four hours, and workshop staff worked from 7am to 4pm on Monday and Tuesday; 7am to 5.45pm on Wednesday, Thursday and Friday; and 7am to 1pm on Saturday.[18] In 1873 a meeting of railway guards and porters was held at the Elephant and Castle Theatre 'to explain to the public the grievances of the railway men and the unjust manner in which some of them are treated.' Some of the men complained that they were required to work 16 to 17 hours per day for a remuneration of 16s 0d per week, and it was noted that the system of overworking and

Plate 21 - London, Chatham & Dover Railway Class R 0-4-4T No.214 and, going out of shot to the left, Martley 0-4-2WT No.98 at Nunhead on 8th July 1899. This class was nicknamed 'large Scotchman'. *Ashford Local Studies Library*

Plate 22 - Upper Sydenham station was opened by the LC&DR in 1884 but is seen here after the formation of the South Eastern & Chatham Railway. One of the water towers of the Crystal Palace is just visible in the hazy distance.   *Lens of Sutton Association*

under-paying railway men was responsible for accidents, and therefore extremely dangerous for the public.[19] Conditions had not improved by 1874, when carriage cleaners and carpenters at Clapham Junction were refused a reduction from fifty-nine to fifty-four hours without wages being proportionately reduced.[20]

Railway managers were often authoritarian when dealing with their employees and the consequent industrial unrest encouraged the development of trade unionism within the companies. However, the London, Chatham & Dover Railway Company was sufficiently far-sighted to offer reasonable wages and working conditions to its staff, and consequently there were few industrial disputes. In his book *The London, Chatham & Dover Railway* Adrian Gray gives the standard wage for a station master in 1858 as 30s 0d a week, and gives the following rates for London, Chatham & Dover staff towards the end of the 19th century:- drivers were earning between 4s 6d to 8s 0d per day, firemen about 4s 0d, firelighters 3s 9d, shed labourers 3s 4d, engine cleaners 2s 0d and carriage-washers from 3s 3d to 4s 4d per day. From 1881 the Company encouraged salaried staff and clerks to contribute to the Railway Clearing House's Superannuation Fund, although no provision was made for manual workers.[21]

In 1884 the London, Chatham & Dover Railway Company opened a new station on the High Level line at Upper Sydenham, and by 1889 the Upper Sydenham station master, Gustavus Farrall, had become Chairman of the 'Railway Guards Universal Friendly Society'. Founded in 1849, this organisation

made provision for widows, orphans and permanently disabled members and by 1889 it had paid a total of £119,688 18s 0½d to claimants. In March 1889 the Victoria district of the London, Chatham & Dover Railway organised a successful concert at the Crystal Palace in aid of the Widows', Orphans, and Permanently Disabled Members Fund of this Society. It was supported by the Prince of Wales, who in the course of a speech said:

*

No public servants deserved their sincere sympathy and support more than the guards of railway trains. It was obvious to all who travelled constantly on railways how much their safety depended on their industry, their vigilance, their sobriety, their discipline, and their exposure to all weathers, and to risks of all kinds.[22]

*

The spiritual needs of railway staff working on the High Level line were catered for by the Railway Mission. This religious organisation held weekly meetings at the May Blossom coffee tavern, Upper Norwood, for railway men working in the locality.[23] The mission was organised by Miss Gurney and Miss Dalton who, assisted by a number of local ladies, sought to convert railway workers to Christianity, whilst warning against the evils of drink. At these meetings the men were usually provided with light refreshments, and after several hymns had been sung they were then encouraged to relate any Christian experiences gained whilst working on the railway. Men who were either unable or unwilling to attend these meetings were often visited at home by Miss Dalton or one of her assistants.

The fact that the mission was organised solely by women was not at all unusual, for there were few opportunities for middle-class women to work during the 19th century. The Victorians considered that a lady was best suited to domesticity, and consequently women were not expected to seek employment. This attitude is summarised in the following quotation '... a lady, to be such, must be a mere lady and nothing else. She must not work for profit, or engage in any occupation that money can command, lest she invade the rights of the working classes.' [24]

It was, however, considered acceptable for women to do charitable work, and philanthropy therefore offered middle-class women the opportunity to play a wider role in society. The popularity of philanthropy is demonstrated by the fact that throughout the 19th century numerous charitable institutions of an evangelical nature appeared.

Some of these were managed exclusively by women, whilst in others women played a major role. Women were not only prominent in the organisation of these charitable institutions, they also contributed financially. It has been estimated that by the end of the 19th century '... about 500,000 women laboured "continuously and semi-professionally" in philanthropy', a statistic which makes the accusation of idleness which was levelled at Victorian women difficult to justify.[25]

Although only a branch line, the High Level railway provided valuable employment for local people throughout the 19th century. The safe working of the line depended upon the vigilance of the guards, drivers, permanent way staff and signalmen, whilst the successful operation of the intermediate stations rested with the station masters and their teams of porters, booking office clerks and ticket inspectors. In addition, the High Level station provided employment for catering staff in the dining and refreshment rooms operated by the catering firm Spiers and Pond, and for bookstall staff, toilet attendants and a number of local cabmen. Booking office staff worked particularly hard as Upper Norwood had become a popular residential district within easy reach of the City, and in the days before the introduction of trams and buses everyone travelled by train. Walter Pellow, who worked in the High Level booking office in the 1890s, was regularly required to stay behind at night, along with the other staff, in order to get 2,000 tickets ready for issue the next morning. Those 2,000 tickets were invariably soon used up. Pellow, who had joined the London, Chatham & Dover Railway at the age of 14, left the High Level station in 1915 for a better post in the office of the London District Chief Engineer. He was eventually appointed station master for West Croydon and Waddon stations.[26]

The stationmaster was perhaps the most highly respected member of the railway hierarchy, since he was responsible for the supervision of other station staff and also represented the interests of the railway company when dealing with its customers. Stationmasters were therefore comparatively well paid and had considerable status within the local community. When Mr J. W. Allen, the stationmaster at the High Level station, died in 1884, the funeral at Honor Oak Cemetery was reported at length in the local press. Mr Allen had served the railway company for 28 years, and it was noted that his funeral was attended by most of the High Level station staff, including Mr Mowle

who ran the station bookstall, and by many other London, Chatham & Dover railwaymen. Amongst those present were Mr Cole, stationmaster at Blackfriars, Mr Ewish, stationmaster at Honor Oak, Mr Bull, stationmaster at Lordship Lane, Mr Stinchcombe, stationmaster at Victoria, Mr Thompson, the outdoor superintendent, Mr Roe, the permanent way inspector, and Mr Renney, the company auditor.[27]

The stationmasters at Honor Oak, Lordship Lane and Upper Sydenham, being responsible for the security of London, Chatham & Dover premises, lived near to their respective stations. Fewer staff were needed to operate the railway in these rural locations but vigilance was still necessary. At Lordship Lane station it was usual for the stationmaster to lock the booking office before going to lunch, but on two occasions during the 19th century thieves climbed over the partition and cleared out the till before making off.[28] Mr Farrall, stationmaster at Upper Sydenham, kept a dog on the premises in order to deter thieves, but in 1889 he was prosecuted by the police 'for

❖

The large villas on Sydenham Hill, such as that depicted in *Plate 4*, provided only a limited number of passengers for the High Level line. The increasing affluence of the area is apparent in these auction details transcribed from a local newspaper advertisement of 1891.

By Messrs. EASTMAN BROTHERS.

"DALKEITH," SYDENHAM RISE.

Close to Lordship Lane Station, L.C. & D.R.

MESSRS. EASTMAN BROTHERS having let the Residence, have received instructions to Sell by Auction on the premises, as above, on WEDNESDAY, March 11th, 1891, at 11 for 12 o'clock punctually, the whole of the excellent FURNITURE and General Effects, comprising brass and japanned iron bedsteads, bedding, blankets, bed and table linen, mahogany wardrobes, chests of drawers, washing tables with marble tops and fittings, Duchesse and other toilet tables and glasses, mahogany cheval glass, night commode, a rosewood drawing room suite upholstered in amber and black tapestry, walnut and mahogany centre, card and occasional tables, rosewood music stand, a brilliant toned grand pianoforte by John Broadwood and Sons in rosewood case, Canterbury whatnot, papier maché occasional chairs, a full compass cottage pianoforte by John Brinsmead and Sons in rosewood case, music stool, brilliant chimney glasses, a 6ft. mahogany enclosed sideboard, set of mahogany extending dining tables, dinner wagon, two mahogany easy and nine dining room chairs, elegant walnut cabinet with silvered plate glass back, well made mahogany bookcase, about 150 vols. of books, water colour drawings, oil paintings, engravings, clocks and ornaments, Brussels carpets, hearthrugs, fender, fire implements, oak hat stand, tapestry and lace curtains, barometer, Chinese gong, linoleum, the contents of the kitchen and offices, china and glass, culinary requisites, iron garden roller, garden seats and numerous other items.

May be viewed on Tuesday, March 10th. Catalogues of the Auctioneer, 23, Bucklersbury, E.C.; and at Forest Hill, Sydenham, and Anerley, S.E.

Plate 23 - A horse bus operated by T. Tilling & Co. outside Nunhead station and destined for Ivydale Road in 1905. This station opened in 1871 but was demolished and rebuilt to the west of Gibbon Road in 1925.   *Southwark Local History Library*

allowing a ferocious dog to be at large without a muzzle'. The summons was dismissed, however, on the grounds that station premises were not covered by the Police Act, as they were the private property of a company.[29]

Sometimes the stationmaster was called upon to deal with an emergency in the locality, as in May 1889 when a man tried to commit suicide by hanging himself from a tree near to the footbridge in Cox's Walk. The man was discovered hanging unconscious from a branch by two platelayers, Simpson and Wilson, who were passing along the High Level railway. They cut him down and immediately sent for Mr Bull, stationmaster of nearby Lordship Lane, who on finding him to be still alive arranged for his transfer to Camberwell Infirmary.[30]

Those aspiring to the position of stationmaster had first to serve their time in the lower ranks, and consequently most men joined the railway company as porters in the hope of eventually achieving a more senior position. Some of the men proved to be most unsuitable employees. In 1871 the residents on Central Hill were greatly annoyed by a prowler who persisted in ringing the house bells at all hours of the night. The culprit was eventually arrested at 1.30am by a policeman from Gipsy Hill police station who identified him as being a porter at the High Level station. For this misdemeanour the porter appeared at the Lambeth police court where he was sentenced to ten days hard labour.[31]

It seems that the porters at the High Level station were also unpopular with the cabmen who operated from a stand outside the station premises in Farquhar Road, for in 1871 the following letter appeared in the *Norwood News*:

*

To The Editor of The Norwood News

Sir, - Believing you are always willing to publish a genuine grievance, I take the liberty, on behalf of myself and other cabmen at the High Level Station, to express a matter which I think only requires publicity to be thoroughly appreciated. For some time past our occupation has been seriously affected by a proceeding which is at once unworthy of the great Company and decidedly unjust towards us. In brief our grievance is this: The porters in the employ of the London Chatham & Dover Railway at the High Level Station have, for some time past, made a practice of acting as outside porters: i.e., carrying, for a small sum, the luggage of the passengers to the various houses in the district, thus depriving us, to a great extent, of our only means of subsistence. Now, sir, this is a great and glaring injustice, for more than one reason. First, we are most of us old inhabitants of Norwood, and therefore our characters for honesty and respectability are such that no possible excuse for this procedure can be assigned on that score. Secondly, some of us are cab proprietors, and therefore it is too bad that, after expending our capital and incurring heavy incidental expenses, we should be interfered with in this manner. Thirdly, it is quite impossible that these Railway servants can properly attend to their own duties while they are making an illegal addition to their salaries by intermeddling with our business. We have appealed in vain to the Railway authorities, and therefore, as a last resource, ask the favour of your kindly inserting this in your next edition. Apologising for thus intruding on your valuable space, I am, Sir, yours, very respectfully,

THE OLDEST NORWOOD CABMAN
On behalf of the other Cabmen

p.s - I should add that great inconvenience is experienced by passengers at the High Level Station, in consequence of the porters being absent, as represented above; the said passengers being thus, in many cases, compelled to carry their own luggage to the train.[32]

*

Guards working on the High Level line were well known and generally liked by the passengers, although it is recorded that trains from the Crystal Palace frequently came to rest on the middle of Blackfriars bridge long enough for the engine driver and guard '... to step out and have a friendly glass', and that this infuriated passengers who had to be in their offices no later than five minutes past nine.[33] A guard was, however, generally recognised as being a responsible individual, and the following obituary, which appeared in 1886, is indicative of the high esteem in which they were held by the travelling public:

*

OBITUARY

We announce with much surprise and regret the death of Joseph Tabor - more widely known as 'Joe the Guard' - for many years a guard on the trains running between High Level station and the City. His pleasant and obliging ways won the esteem and admiration of all who knew him, and his cheery face will be much missed by passengers to the City and intermediate stations along the High Level route.[34]

*

One enterprising London, Chatham and Dover guard left his job and used the reputation he had gained whilst working on the High Level line to set up his own coal business, collecting orders from an office at the High Level station.[35]

The work of the guard could also be hazardous. It is recorded that on the 4th December 1878 the body of Francis Kelly, the guard on the last train to leave for Crystal Palace from Victoria, was found in the tunnel near to the High Level station. Kelly was on board the train when it left Lordship Lane station, but presumably he leant against the door of the guard's van when it was not properly closed and fell out, for when the train arrived at the Crystal Palace terminus the door was found to be open.[36]

Guards were also very often the first persons to discover the bodies of prematurely born infants. In November 1887 a Mr Forder was the guard on the 9.37am train from Victoria which arrived at the High Level station at 10.20am. Whilst inspecting the carriages, he found a parcel under a seat in a third class carriage, and on examination this proved to be the dead body of a newly born male child.[37] The frequent occurrence of such incidents on the High Level line during the 19th century can be attributed to the strict moral values of the Victorian age. It was not acceptable for a woman to give birth to a child outside of marriage, so consequently a pregnant single woman could

expect to be strongly condemned and ostracised by society.

In September 1872 the lamplighter at the High Level station, who was required to work night shifts, figured prominently in the local newspapers in connection with an attempted burglary at Marlborough House in nearby Farquhar Road. Whilst on duty at 4am one morning the lamplighter heard cries of "police" and "murder" coming from the direction of the house. Upon investigating he was confronted with the spectacle of a man carrying a dagger in one hand and a revolver in the other who was bleeding from a wound in the leg and wearing a shirt which was saturated in blood. However, the man soon identified himself as Delfin Soria, a Spanish servant who had temporarily been left in charge of Marlborough House. Soria had become involved in a fight with four men who were attempting to carry out a burglary and had managed to shoot one of the burglars before being stabbed by another. Convinced that the man he had shot was dead, Soria and the lamplighter promptly re-entered the premises only to find that all of the burglars had escaped, leaving the hall floor smothered in blood. The police were subsequently able follow a trail of the blood across two gardens and a large plot of vacant grass land, but the injured man obviously stopped to tie up his wound, for the trail of blood abruptly stopped. None of the burglars was apprehended.[38]

THE HAZARDS OF 19TH CENTURY RAIL TRAVEL

The growth of the Victorian railway network was accompanied by numerous accidents. Maintenance was often inadequate and the installation of effective braking and signalling equipment proceeded slowly in most areas. Many of the companies had acute financial problems which prevented the introduction of new equipment, and in any case rivalry between railway companies often prevented one company from adopting any successful measure introduced by another.

The problem of railway safety had been addressed as early as 1841, when a Select Committee on Railways investigated the possibility of granting the Board of Trade supervisory powers over the railway companies in order to prevent accidents. However, the railway companies argued against discretionary powers being given to the Board of Trade because any division of responsibility between the company and the Board of Trade '... would be injurious to the management of the company, and would be detrimental to the interests of the public.'

This view was accepted by the Select Committee and consequently the final report recommended that the Board of Trade should exercise supervision '... in the way of suggestion rather than in that of positive regulation.' [39] This, of course, did little to improve safety standards.

Such was the frequency of railway accidents in Victorian times that *The Railway Traveller's Handy Book* gave the following advice to passengers:

*

HOW TO ACT IN CASES OF THREATENED ACCIDENTS

When the train comes to a sudden standstill at an unaccustomed stopping-place, it is usually a sign that there is something amiss; but this something may be of very trivial moment. At all events, do not vex yourself with the idea incessantly that catastrophes are about to occur, nor pester the guard with questions only to receive ambiguous and evasive replies. If an absolute stoppage takes place, the best plan is to quit the carriage, and then whatever may occur you will be safe. In cases where the carriages are felt to be overturning, there is but one method, and that is to jump from the upper side as the carriages go over, and in taking this jump the feet should be placed close together, the arms held close to the side, and the body inclined forwards.

Many concussions give no warning of their approach, while others do, the usual premonitory symptoms being a kind of bouncing or leaping of the train. It is well to know that the bottom of the carriage is the safest place, and therefore, when a person has reason to anticipate a concussion, he should, without hesitation, throw himself upon the floor of the carriage.[40]

*

In December 1882, following the collapse of a railway bridge in Bromley which killed several people, a letter appeared in the *Norwood Review & Crystal Palace Reporter* complaining about the general condition of bridges on the London, Chatham & Dover Railway. The writer called for an independent examination of all bridges belonging to the company, pointing out that re-painting was infrequent, and that many of the bolts in use were rusty. Commenting on the practice of keeping trains waiting either on or under bridges he stated that '... I always feel somewhat nervous at the great vibrations caused by passing trains'.[41]

Less than eighteen months later a major bridge collapse did occur, and although the bridge was owned by the London, Brighton & South Coast Railway, a London, Chatham & Dover engine, travelling back from the Crystal Palace, was involved. The local press reported the accident thus:

*

FALL OF A RAILWAY BRIDGE

A curious accident, fortunately unattended with either loss of life or serious injury to any person, though involving great delay to traffic and inconvenience, happened early on Thursday morning near Denmark Hill Station, when a portion of a bridge crossing the line, without any warning, fell in, and was immediately run into by an engine. The bridge in question is situated in Camberwell Grove, and is at the Peckham end of a short tunnel outside Denmark Hill Station. At this point there are four lines of rails, two forming the Crystal Palace and Blackheath branch of the London Chatham & Dover Railway, and the others the Victoria and London Bridge section of the London Brighton & South Coast Railway Company. Both lines are the property of the last named, the Chatham Company only having running powers. For some time past the bridge has been under supervision and four of the girders spanning the London Bridge lines had been removed, while four others that showed flaws had been shored up. On the Chatham Company's side, however,

close examination by the engineers had failed to disclose any flaw.

The last down train from Ludgate Hill passed at half past twelve, and the engine that took this train to the Crystal Palace returned "light" to the Chatham and Dover sheds at Stewart's Lane, Battersea. It was as nearly as possible one o'clock when it reached the bridge just as four of the girders fell in with the roadway above. The engine, one of the ordinary "tanks" with a storm shelter, was running at a good pace, and without warning plunged into the fallen mass of iron and concrete almost burying itself, and throwing the whole of the wheels off the metals. Luckily neither driver nor fireman were hurt, and were able to draw their fire, remaining at their engine until the morning.

An alarm was at once given, and Mr Rhodes, the station master, who was speedily on the spot, telegraphed to London for assistance. A break down gang and about 150 men were soon sent down, and under the superintendence of Mr J. P. Knight, the general manager, and Mr Richardson, the superintendent, got to work to clear away the debris. The total weight of iron that fell was about twenty tons, and the roadway and concrete would be about ten or fifteen tons more. Had the bridge fallen half an hour earlier, just as the loaded train was running down, the consequences might have been very serious. The driver and fireman of the engine also had a narrow escape, for had they been running tender first they would almost certainly have been killed or severely injured.

This cutting has, we believe, been a constant trouble and expense to the company, some thousands of pounds having been spent in securing the bank. Considerable consternation and inconvenience was experienced by those who use the line for the City. Persons in Upper Norwood, not having heard of the accident, kept arriving at the High Level Station to find that they must either go by the low level or Sydenham Hill. It was not until between five and six o'clock on Thursday evening that the traffic was resumed.[42]

*

Derailments were often caused by permanent way defects, particularly at points. Such accidents frequently caused severe delays and sometimes resulted in fatalities.

On Saturday, 21st May 1881 at 11.48am a train from Victoria left the rails whilst entering the High Level station. The front carriage fell right over on its side and the carriage following behind was tilted sideways. The train, which consisted of the engine, a break and ten carriages, was travelling at six miles per hour when the wheels of the front carriage left the rails at points. The driver, when questioned, stated that he had already passed over the same points twice that day.

It was at first thought that the guard was the only casualty, as he was found to have fractured ribs. However, when the wreckage was searched the body of a young boy was discovered under the footboard attached to the centre compartment. The boy was travelling with a bag containing carrier pigeons, and the birds were therefore released with notes tied to their legs

Plate 24 - The crew pose for this photograph of LC&DR Kirtley 0-4-4T No.166 at Crystal Palace High Level station in the 1890s. The station was the scene of a number of mishaps, described in the text.

Roger Carpenter

which read 'Crystal Palace High Level - Your boy has met with an accident: come at once'. Three hours later Mr H. Stubbimgs arrived from Plumstead and identified his son Henry, age 12.[43]

A less serious derailment occurred when a light engine left the rails whilst shunting on the London, Chatham & Dover line near Nunhead in November 1889. The accident caused considerable damage, resulting in great inconvenience to passengers. At Ludgate Hill station the platforms and booking office were crowded with people who were forced to wait until the damage to the track had been sufficiently repaired to enable trains to proceed along the Crystal Palace, the Blackheath, and the Greenwich lines.[44]

In 1863 the London, Chatham & Dover Railway employed William Robert Sykes as its signals engineer. Sykes soon gained the railway company a reputation for reliable signalling equipment, and his own reputation was further enhanced when he invented a 'lock and block' system in which the train controlled the block instrument, and the block instrument was interlocked with the outdoor signals. The Board of Trade inspectors approved of the idea, and by 1882 the 'lock and block' system was installed on most of the Chatham's lines.[45] However, despite the introduction of this equipment, two accidents occurred on the High Level line which were both due to signalling errors.

On Monday, 13th December 1886 a City train was loading at platform 1 of the High Level station when a collision occurred.

A passenger who was on the platform gave this account of the accident:

*

I was an eye-witness of an accident which occurred on Monday morning at the Crystal Palace Station of the London Chatham & Dover Railway. I was on the platform at the time, and about to take my seat in the train to start for the City, when I saw at the other end of the station a train emerging from under the East Station archway on the same line of rail, with the whistle blowing hard. It was no sooner noticed than it ran with considerable violence into the train about to start, smashing the framework of the first carriage of this train, and breaking a great number of the windows. The passengers in the incoming train were much shaken. The driver of the engine that had brought in the train about to start had a miraculous escape. He was on the ground attending to the forward part of his engine, and had just barely passed in front of it, when the collision occurred. He appears to have been knocked aside by the buffer of his engine, and fell between it and the platform, but it is believed without being much hurt.[46]

*

The second accident was potentially far more serious, although no lives were lost. It occurred on Monday, 16th November 1891 at Upper Sydenham station, whilst a goods train was standing at the down platform of the station unloading coal with its two

Plate 25 - LC&DR A1 Class 0-4-4T at Lordship Lane heading a train of oil-lit carriages, probably in the 1890s. Included for its historical interest, this is another poor exposure, not helped by the smoke from the locomotive drifting lazily across to the other platform.

Kent Libraries and Archives

break vans still within the tunnel. An empty passenger train was signalled through at Lordship Lane, and although vision in the tunnel was obscured by smoke, this train entered at full speed before the driver was aware that there was anything on the line in front of him. In the resulting collision the break vans were completely wrecked and they blocked the up line for over six hours. The driver and fireman of the passenger train had a narrow escape.[47]

It is unlikely that the engines which caused these two accidents were fitted with the Westinghouse braking system, as it is evident that both drivers were unable to stop in time. By 1884 the London, Chatham & Dover company had adopted the Westinghouse brake but it was only fitted to a few of their main line trains. The majority of the trains were still not provided with any form of continuous brake.[48]

The High Level station was the scene of two further accidents which both resulted in fatalities. On Saturday, 11th August 1888 it was reported that William Field, a cabman at the station, climbed over a wall near to the station entrance and fell through a glass roof onto the stone floor opposite the booking office. Robert Grout the station master and Walter Wickenden, who was employed at the bookstall, both heard the crash of glass but they were unable to assist as the cabman was killed instantly by the fall.[49]

In November 1890 another death occurred when a boiler which had been removed from the machinery shed at the Crystal Palace was being hoisted onto a wagon in the station yard. The chain supporting the boiler suddenly gave way, causing it to fall onto one of the labourers who was assisting. He was killed on the spot, and it is recorded that the crushed remains were taken by the police to Camberwell Mortuary.[50]

There was also another fatal accident in 1890. This occurred at Nunhead station, when David Burns, a labourer, was killed on the railway line. The signalman at Nunhead Junction signal box gave details of the accident at the subsequent inquest:

*

He saw the deceased at work on the siding off the down line unloading a truck of flints. At 1.48 the witness signalled the line clear for the 1.50 express from Victoria

to the Crystal Palace. A minute later he heard the train nearing the station, the driver blowing his whistle most furiously. On looking out of his box the witness saw the deceased walking along the line between the rails and the platform. Deceased took no heed of the whistle at first, but in a moment he seemed suddenly to realise his position, and he ran for his life. He was too late, however; the buffer of the engine caught him, hurled him forward about 12 yards, and then the unfortunate man fell, with his head on the outer rail, and every wheel on that side of the train passed over him. The deceased had no business where he was, and, as a curve in the line was close at hand, he and the driver of the train were not in each other's view until they were close together. He could not explain why the deceased was on the line, but he did not think he contemplated suicide.[51]

*

Railway lines have always proved to be irresistible to children and the High Level line was no exception. To the annoyance of engine drivers children regularly ran across the line, gaining access by either climbing over fences, or getting through convenient gaps. This dangerous pastime often resulted in death or serious injury.

On Saturday, 2nd June 1888 an inquest was held at the George & Dragon in St Georges Road, Camberwell, on the bodies of two boys who met their deaths on the railway near Honor Oak. One death had occurred on a Thursday and the other on a Friday afternoon. The proceedings were opened by the coroner who remarked that '... those who believe in coincidence may be interested to learn that the two children were both killed by the 4.42 express from the Palace.'

The first boy, a 10-year-old, was killed when he visited Nunhead fields with several other children to pick buttercups. The children ran across the railway line and climbed an embankment, but the 10-year-old tripped and fell in front of the 4.42pm train from Crystal Palace to Aldersgate. The driver, William Clarke, said that he did not see the boys as they were obscured by the passing of an up train to the Palace, about midway between Nunhead and Honor Oak. He confirmed that there was no roadway across the fields which were on either side of the line, however, '... every day there are children running about on the metals. I have to be always using my whistle to get them out of the way.'

The second death occurred when a 9-year-old boy dropped his hat on the rails whilst visiting Nunhead fields. He attempted to recover it, but was killed by a passing train from Crystal Palace. The 4.42pm was an express which did not stop at Honor Oak, and consequently when it reached Nunhead fields it was travelling at too great a speed to allow the driver to stop.

Although a verdict of accidental death was reached in both cases, Inspector Josiah Rae of the London, Chatham & Dover company was questioned about the safety of the section of permanent way between Nunhead and Honor Oak stations. (An 8-year-old boy, the son of a signalman, had been killed on the line four years earlier, and at the inquest it had been pointed out that the spot ought to be better protected.[52]) Inspector Rae stated that on either side of the line there were post and rail fences, and that there were no access points near to the scene of the two accidents. The fences had been tarred to deter children, but this had proved to be ineffective. Notice boards which had been erected and painted two years before had been damaged by children who threw stones at them.[53]

Goods trains frequently travelled up and down the High Level line and these were often targeted by children. A description of their activities is given in *Forest Hill* by Doris Pullen:

*

They used to bowl their hoops over London Road to the alleyway running at the bottom of Horniman's Park. They would take an old sack with them, for the trucks used to come along the railway track there from Lordship Lane station, and at times these were piled so high with coal that great lumps would fly over the railings onto the alleyway, and these were gathered up by the children and taken home. One day they found a chicken running along the alleyway that had escaped from a goods train which used to go to the markets every morning filled with livestock. They tried to catch it to take it home for a pet, but it got away.[54]

*

The division between Protestant and Catholic in Ireland gave rise to terrorist activity on the railways in 1884 when an attempt was made to detonate large quantities of dynamite at Victoria, Charing Cross, Paddington and Ludgate Hill stations. Fortunately only one explosion occurred at Victoria station and this resulted in £4,000 worth of damage.[55] A placard offering £2,000 reward for the apprehension of the terrorists was widely circulated, and as a precaution all luggage deposited in the cloak rooms of London railway stations was scrutinised. Many of the stationmasters at local stations were quick to adopt the same procedure.

Shortly after the explosion at Victoria station, a rumour was circulated that two men had been arrested for attempting to blow up the Crystal Palace. Although this proved to be untrue, it was reported that extra precautions were taken by the police authorities at that time due to a rumour that the Crystal Palace was to be the next target.[56]

VICTORIAN PASSENGERS

Throughout the latter part of the 19th century there were frequent complaints about the condition of the carriages in use on the High Level line, and about the punctuality of Chatham and Dover trains. In February 1880 the *Norwood Review and Crystal Palace Reporter* published a list of complaints from a London, Chatham and Dover first class season ticket holder:

*

A FEW THINGS THE DIRECTORS OF THE LCDR COMPANY MIGHT LIKE TO KNOW

'... that in the bitterest cold of winter, they have never been guilty of tarnishing the virgin purity of their carriages with even a single foot warmer'.

'... that in cold weather all sensible ladies travel by another line instead, which has had the sense to provide foot warmers'.

'... that to provide locomotives to run in the middle of winter without any headshield to protect the stoker and engine driver from the keen blasts which blow in their teeth as they are on the lookout for signals, renders them liable to have an action brought against them by the Society for the Prevention of Cruelty to Animals'.

'... that they have so carefully arranged the times of the City trains that unless a passenger starts from his house in Upper Norwood at the absurd time (for a gentleman) of ten minutes to eight in the morning to catch the 8.5, he never by any chance steps on to the platform at Aldersgate Street until a quarter past nine'.

'... that the 8.32 train is so overcrowded at Loughboro' Junction, through so many previous stoppages, that there is rarely standing room in the second class nor sitting room in the first class carriages while the contemporaneous train from Bickley is nearly empty'.

'... that there are highly respectable people living within a mile from the Crystal Palace who have been seduced into buying a season ticket to travel on the LCDR line through several conspicuous advertisements fixed to the towers of the aforesaid Company's station, which inform a simple minded and confiding public that not only are there frequent trains to the City every hour, but that these trains convey the trusting passenger in twenty minutes to his destination at Holborn'.

'... that instead of frequent trains every hour, there are only thirty trains in the twenty-four hours, and so far from taking only twenty minutes over the journey, the quickest train, as booked in their time-tables, takes twenty-three minutes, while only six trains in the day are authorised to take less than half an hour, while the others are authorised to take more'.

'... that when nearly every railway company in Great Britain makes use of continuous brakes, that passengers prefer going by those trains on which the Directors have not been slow to take advantage of the benefits to time and safety conferred by those inventions'.

'... that continuous brakes are conspicuous on their line chiefly by their absence'.

'... that at present the burners of the LCDR company resemble the lamps in an Esquimaux snow hut as regards power of illumination'. [57]

*

However, conditions on the High Level line did not significantly improve, and complaints from disgruntled passengers continued to be published throughout the 1880s.

*

Many times have the public entreated to be allowed windows in the 2nd class carriages that will remain shut in the drifting sleet of winter; but it is of no use. The shareholders' money is poured like water into the Thames in the form of stone and iron; but the rolling stock is shamefully neglected .... I daily carry a small oak wedge in my waistcoat pocket; and when I have put the window up, I hold it in my left hand while I push the wedge tightly between the window and the carriage and have thus obtained some degree of comfort for myself.

The timings of their trains can only properly be compared with the weather prophecies in Old Moore's Almanac i.e. 'Day before or day after'. I heard on official authority that on the last Bank Holiday but one, a train returning from Margate to Victoria, and due at the Crystal Palace at 8 oclock in the evening, arrived at four the next morning.

I have been in the habit of leaving Ludgate by the 7.15 train in the evening, and changing at Nunhead and coming on to the Palace by a Victoria train. Three or four months ago we had been some ten minutes or more late every night in arriving for a long time, when, by some interposition of Providence, the train reached the Palace exact to time on one occasion; and so utterly unprepared were the attendants for such an unheard of event, that all the passengers carried their tickets out with them, there being nobody at the gate to receive them. [58]

... the whole service of trains on the line to the Palace, their speed and appointments, are as bad as bad can be... To comment upon the carriages is needless. Everybody knows that they are dirty, draughty, uncomfortable and of the oldest and most wretched type. Is it any wonder that so many houses in this neighbourhood are empty, and that Norwood is rapidly falling into disfavour as a place of residence. [59]

*

Despite the number of complaints about the High Level line, passengers continued to travel to the Crystal Palace. In 1886

the London, Chatham and Dover Company announced that a special express train would leave from Victoria at 5.10pm every Wednesday and Saturday to enable people to visit the outdoor fetes at the Palace. [60] Visitors were also encouraged to make use of its evening facilities. Advertisements informed them that they could dine in the grand saloon whilst witnessing the illumination of the grounds, which were particularly impressive, as almost fifty acres were lit up by over 50,000 gas and oil lamps. Visitors could then enjoy an open air ballet - the 'Sculptor's Vision', before returning to Victoria in twenty-five minutes on a special train run by the Chatham and Dover company from the High Level station. [61]

Facilities at the High Level station were designed to impress the first time visitor. Class consciousness in Victorian times ensured that railway passengers were strictly segregated, so facilities had to be duplicated so that those travelling first class could have access to their own waiting rooms, refreshment rooms and booking offices. Consequently, at the High Level station there was a separate platform for first class passengers, and from this platform an underground passage led from the station to the Crystal Palace, enabling the passengers to gain direct access to the first class entrance in the centre transept. [62] It was also usual for Victorian railway companies to marshal first class compartments near the centre of trains so that their patrons could wait under the shelter of the platform canopies and also be better placed to escape injury in the event of a collision. These facilities no doubt proved useful to the many members of the nobility who visited the Palace over the years, including perhaps Queen Victoria, who apparently preferred the High Level line because she had an aversion to the lengthy Penge tunnel under Sydenham Hill. [63]

However, the Palace attracted people of all social classes, and on the popular one shilling fete days the masses descended upon the area, much to the annoyance of local people. Costermongers' barrows lined the pavements and on one occasion '... a lad having been sent out to sprinkle chloride of lime about, owing to the obnoxious odours arising from whelks, fried fish, and oil burners, was freely missiled with such things as oyster shells, ginger beer bottles etc.'

As an aggrieved resident observed, 'A few more half-guinea and five shilling days might prove an additional attraction to that select class which does not care to mingle with the vulgar shilling crowd.' [64]

Sometimes passengers travelling in second and third class railway carriages caused a considerable amount of damage, and inconvenience.

*

Among other dirty tricks they practise, are putting their dirty boots upon the cushion of the opposite seat; knocking out their pipe ashes anywhere, on seat, arm-rest or window ledge; with unlimited spitting on the floor. To these things some of them add the amiable amusement of cutting the cushions, scratching their name upon the windows, or obliterating any notice that may be put up in the carriage. [65]

*

Plate 26 - A Down London, Chatham & Dover Railway train at Lordship Lane, probably during the 1890s. A sylvan setting at this time but still the scene of a daylight robbery when Mrs Hocker was attacked. The assault is described on the next page.   *Gary Cross*

The unruly and often unsavoury characters that the Palace attracted sometimes caused trouble at the High Level station. On Thursday, 6th October 1880 upwards of 200 young men were seen to roam about the Crystal Palace building in gangs of five or six shouting, flourishing sticks and pushing people in a rough manner. The subsequent press report noted that '... some 150 of the disorderly mob then proceeded to Messrs Spiers and Pond's refreshment bar in the High Level railway station. Here they commenced a most disgraceful disturbance. The manager stopped the sale of all liquors and, with the aid of some 30 constables the bar was cleared, but business had to be entirely suspended. The crowd then rushed down the steps on to the railway platform, and the riotous conduct was continued. Again the services of the police had to be obtained, and after a great deal of difficulty the platform was cleared and the mob driven into the roadway.'[66]

The Spiers and Pond refreshment bar was obviously a place to avoid, for in June 1881 a Mr T. Quartermaine accidently discharged a single barrelled revolver in the bar. The ball struck a gold ring on his little finger, passed through the fleshy part of his right hand, and afterwards struck the ceiling. It was reported that considerable consternation and alarm was caused, and that the loss of blood was very great.[67] A further riot occurred in the refreshment bar in 1884, following a firework display at the Palace. On this occasion the police had to clear the premises and bolt the doors of the railway station in order to prevent any further trouble. Five of the principal rioters were subsequently taken into custody.[68]

The High Level station was also frequented by pickpockets whenever any major event took place at the Palace. Returning home from a firework display one passenger, a Mr Farr, was standing on a crowded platform when he felt a hand enter his trouser pocket. He managed to apprehend the pickpocket who, when subsequently searched, was found to have four £20 notes, a £5 note, and a large quantity of gold and silver.[69]

At night passengers using Farquhar Road to gain access to the High Level station were sometimes solicited by women who waited near to the station entrance. This prompted one angry resident to complain about the matter to the local press.

*

A DISGRACE

Sir,

Will you allow me a small space in your issue to air what is considered by many a standing nuisance. People who use the High Level station are constantly, after nightfall, annoyed and importuned by a group of women who habitually stand along the approach. Only last Thursday on coming from town with two lady friends, our ears were saluted by a string of the foulest language, which came from two of them who were quarreling.

I maintain, and am endorsed by many, that this is a disgrace to the neighbourhood. I enclose my card

I remain, yours faithfully,[70]

*

Passengers using other stations on the High Level line also experienced the occasional problem. In a letter to the local press Nunhead station was described by one unfortunate passenger as '... this Godforsaken hole, dignified by the name of station'. The writer complained about the minimal facilities for waiting passengers, and concluded his letter by commenting that 'In addition to the discomfort and dangers of waiting, the demeanour of the company's officials is most offensive'. [71]

On a foggy November evening in 1890 a woman was attacked in the subway of Lordship Lane station whilst making her way to the platform. Her assailant attempted to steal her purse but was deterred by the woman's screams. Following the attempted robbery, the woman's brother wrote to the *Sydenham and Penge Gazette* claiming that his sister had subsequently identified her assailant as John Thompson, a cabman who had a stand at the station. This accusation severely damaged Thompson's reputation and had an adverse effect upon his business. It was later proved that Thompson could not have been the culprit as he was nowhere near the station at the time of the robbery. [72]

A second robbery occurred in July 1895, which was witnessed by passengers in a passing train:

*

Highway robbery of the most daring character was perpetrated at Lordship Lane in broad day light on Saturday evening. Mrs Hocker, of Highclere, Westwood Park, Forest Hill, was coming down the footpath leading from Westwood Park to Lordship Lane about 5 o'clock on her way to the station and when near what is locally known as "the Kissing-gate" which leads into the roadway, she was attacked by a man whose object it was at once evident, was robbery. Mrs Hocker struggled with her assailant, but was thrown down and her gold watch and chain were taken from her. She managed, however, to protect her purse and bracelet. No one seems to have been within call at the time and the man got away. The attack, however, was witnessed by the people in a down train that was running into the station, and one of the passengers informed the station master, who immediately ran to the spot where he found Mrs Hocker in a very distressed condition. No trace, however, of her assailant was discovered, and there seems to be little hope of his arrest. [73]

*

The predominantly rural setting of the High Level line in Victorian times made it attractive not only to those wishing to commit robberies, but also to those wishing to commit suicide. Many of the incidents were in the vicinity of Lordship Lane and Honor Oak stations, and these were extensively reported in the local press.

In May 1893 Arthur Barnes was driving the 3.30am goods train to the Crystal Palace when, as he approached Lordship Lane station, he noticed the severed body of a woman on the track in front of his engine. An investigation revealed that the woman had been seen the previous evening by one of the porters. She had asked to be allowed to go into the waiting-room, but was not seen to leave. She had also been seen several times on the previous day walking up and down the pathway which ran alongside the railway. The only other train to pass before the 3.30am goods train was the 12.7am train from Holborn to the Crystal Palace. However, the driver when questioned said that the morning was foggy and that consequently he saw nothing. The engine was examined but no marks were found upon it. [74]

Sometimes the reason for the suicide became apparent when the body of the deceased was subsequently searched. In January 1895 a man threw himself in front of the 9.22am train from the Crystal Palace as it approached the Cox's Walk footbridge near to Lordship Lane station. In one of his overcoat pockets a piece of paper was found giving his name and address together with the statement 'I am going blind; cannot see to do my work; love to all'. [75]

The death of a passenger sometimes occurred by accident, as in the case of a commercial traveller who was seen walking near the edge of the Up platform on Honor Oak station in May 1895. A train was entering the station at the time, and the man was seen to suddenly lose his balance and fall against the front of the engine. The body was caught by the rod coupling the wheels of the engine and was hurled back onto the platform. [76]

It was, however, possible to be hit by a train and still survive. Thomas Whiffen was a ticket collector at the High Level station. In December 1893 he had the following lucky escape:

*

He was in the act of crossing the rails between the signal box and the station, when he noticed the approach of a train, which he took to be the one due at 10.16am, and which is drawn up at No.2 platform. If this had been so he could have avoided it. But it really was the 10.18 train from Victoria which goes to platform No.3. Whiffen did not observe this soon enough to get clear of it, though he made an attempt. According to his own statement, he then gave himself up as lost. He remembers one of the buffers of the engine striking him, and nothing more, for he then lost consciousness. However, he was knocked into the six-foot way where he lay till he was picked up, placed in a cab, and quickly taken to the Norwood Cottage Hospital. A medical examination revealed a dislocated shoulder, broken ribs, and a severe wound on the arm. The patient is making satisfactory progress. [77]

*

A strange incident occurred in September 1886, when it was feared that a young girl had been killed at Upper Sydenham station. A woman was seen to rush frantically along the platform declaring that her daughter had jumped from the train while it was passing through the tunnel between the High Level and Upper Sydenham stations. A search was instantly carried out but no trace of the missing girl was found. The woman was left behind at Upper Sydenham; however, when the train arrived at Brixton the guard was informed by another passenger that the girl had been found. Apparently the girl and her mother had caught the 5.33pm train from the High Level station on the day in question. While going through the tunnel the girl, without making any noise, succeeded in climbing over the backs of the seats to reach the far end of the compartment where she hid until she was discovered at Brixton. [78]

❖

Plate 27 - Honor Oak station perched on the embankment. This view was possibly taken in 1897 when a photographer was on hand to record a demonstration that took place against the construction of a private golf course. In 1896 Honor Oak Hill had been enclosed by a company who wished to turn it into a private golf course and resisted the efforts of a protest committee. The golfers suggested that the work would provide 'the people' with desirable sports facilities. 'The people' were not impressed, resulting in some 15,000 people demonstrating over two weekends in October 1897. Regrettably, those photographs are too poor to be reproduced.

John Stanton collection

❀ Pictorial survey - Honor Oak ❀

Plate 28 - Honor Oak in 1949. Obvious changes from pre-1925 days are the addition of the third rail and cable runs associated with electrification of the branch. The wooden planked platforms were typical of the line until they were extended by the Southern Railway when the extensions were engineered in the Southern's usual style. Less visible are the changes to the platform lamps; indeed, the lamp under the awning appears to be illuminated by gas - the 'pull cord' is hanging down. However, there is still only a solitary passenger.   *Mike Morant*

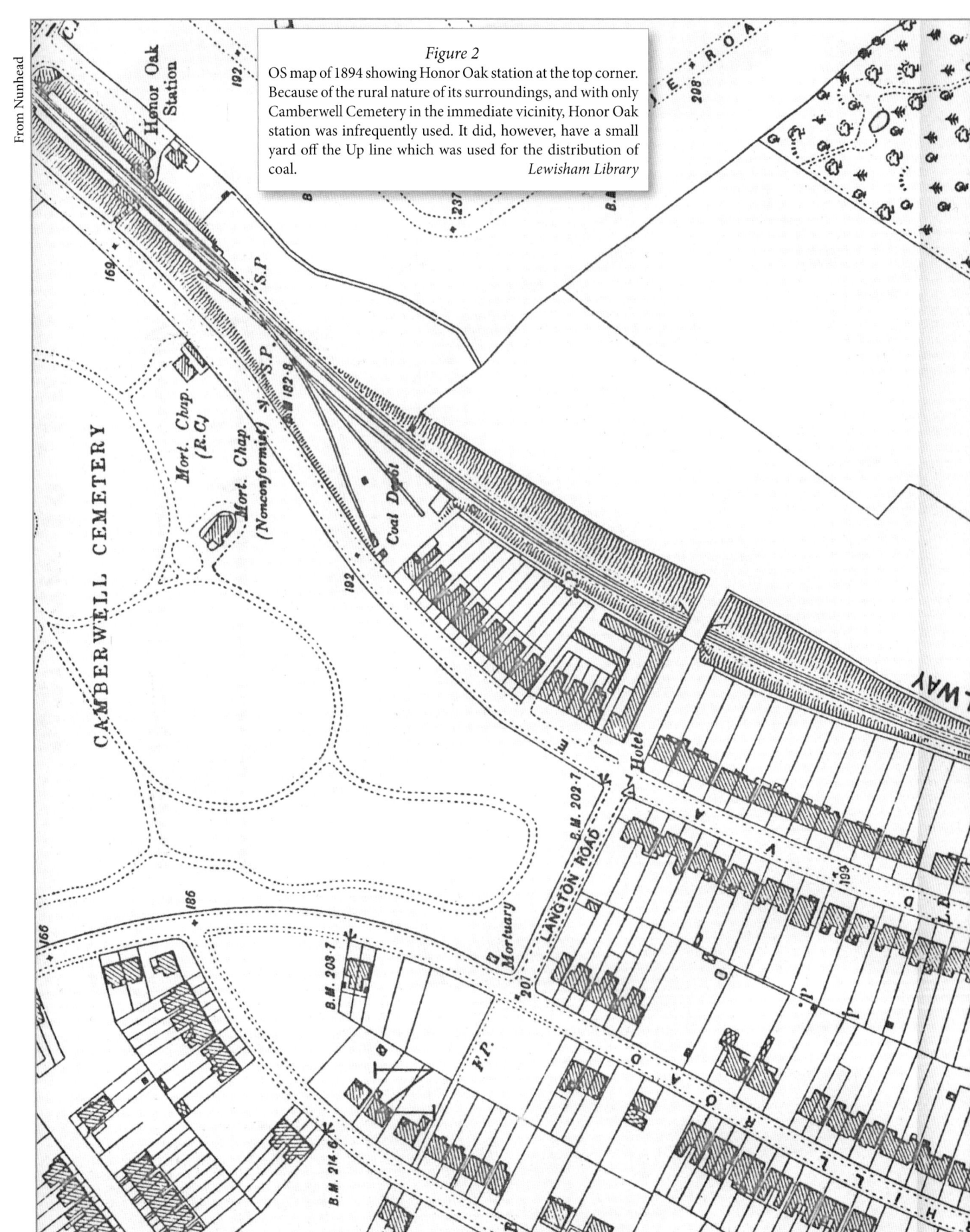

Figure 2
OS map of 1894 showing Honor Oak station at the top corner.
Because of the rural nature of its surroundings, and with only
Camberwell Cemetery in the immediate vicinity, Honor Oak
station was infrequently used. It did, however, have a small
yard off the Up line which was used for the distribution of
coal.
Lewisham Library

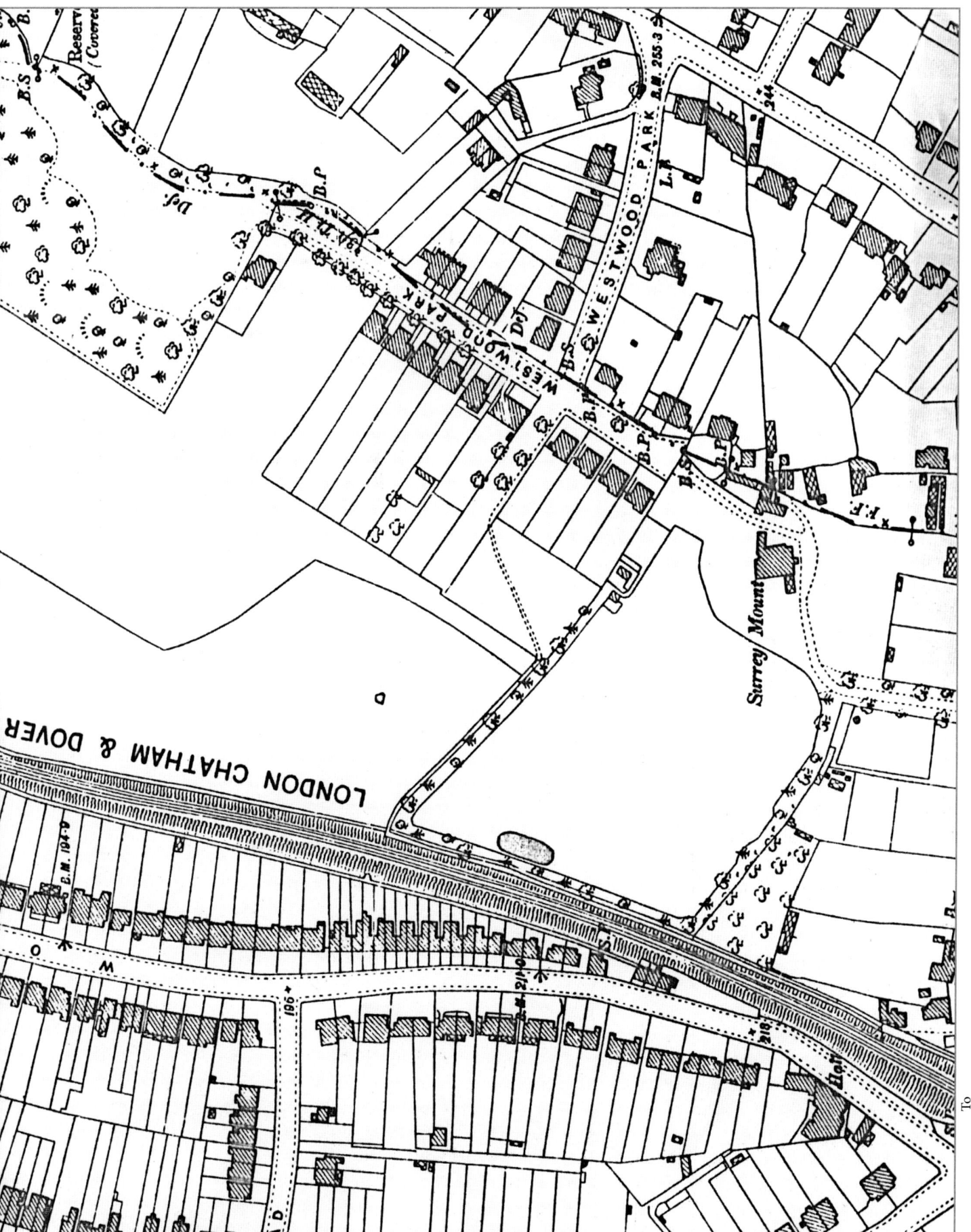

To
Lordship Lane

Plate 29 - The coal yard sidings at Honor Oak station taken from the Down platform, which has been extended at the signal box end to accommodate longer trains.   *Denis Cullum*

17th September 1954, the penultimate day of the passenger service

Plate 30 - View of an unkempt Honor Oak from the coal yard. The opposite platform has been extended using the Southern-style concrete construction. Note the rail-built support for the two loading gauges spanning two of the sidings.   *Denis Cullum*

Plate 31 - The station from the coal yard entrance affording a good view of the signal box and the construction detail of the platform extension that enveloped it as electrification was introduced. *Lens of Sutton Association*

Plate 32 - Honor Oak platforms and waiting shelters, looking towards Lordship Lane from the Up platform. The wooden platforms are accentuated in this view whilst the station running-in board has fallen to the ground. 17th September 1954. *Denis Cullum*

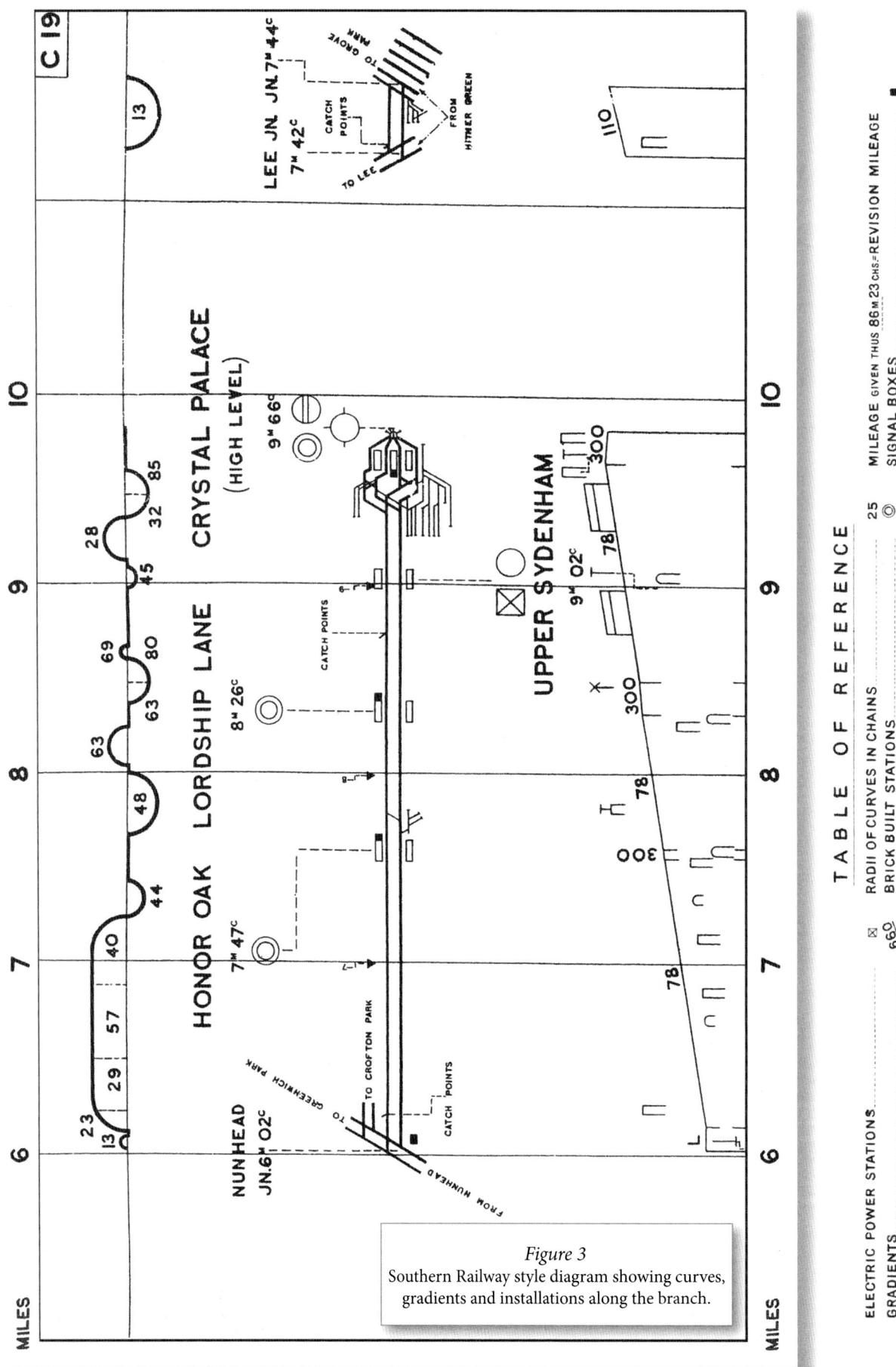

Figure 3
Southern Railway style diagram showing curves,
gradients and installations along the branch.

❧ *Chapter Four* ❧

THE SOUTH EASTERN & CHATHAM RAILWAY

The fares levied by the London, Chatham & Dover Railway on the High Level line were a source of constant complaint during the 1880s. This was a potentially serious situation, as the complaints occurred at a time when the Crystal Palace was beginning to lose its popularity with the public due to the availability of alternative amusements. Although the line was used by commuters travelling to and from the City, visitors to the Crystal Palace were still a valuable source of income for the railway company, and it would therefore have been advisable to make some concession to public demand. The high fares were, however, maintained, and this eventually resulted in a reduction in the number of passengers using the line.

✳

The casual visitor to the district by the High Level route must be struck by the paucity of the travelling public, as evidenced in the large number of trains but scantily filled, and indeed, totally empty carriages, observable at all hours of the day. This state of things is to be attributed more or less directly to the heavy fares, and is the result of an illiberal use made of an important monopoly, affecting a district so situated naturally that it cannot readily resort to those ordinary contrivances which it is the good fortune of other districts to have provided for them.[1]

✳

The declining popularity of the Crystal Palace led the Chairman of the Crystal Palace Company to approach both of the railway companies serving the area with a request to reduce fares for Bank Holiday visitors. The measure proved to be successful, and at a shareholders meeting held at the City Terminus Hotel Cannon Street on 16th August 1881 the Chairman was able to report that 8,000 additional visitors had travelled to the Palace on the previous Bank Holiday.[2] However, the railway companies made no further concessions to the Crystal Palace Company, and consequently in March 1883 a public meeting was held at Queen's Hall, Forest Hill, in order to consider petitioning Parliament for the construction of a railway to be called the 'East of London, Crystal Palace, and South Eastern Junction Railway'.

Mr Mungo McGeorge, the Chairman of the Crystal Palace Company, presided over the meeting at the Queen's Hall. He said that they had met for the purpose of promoting increased railway accommodation in the neighbourhood. It was forty-two years since the Brighton Railway opened up the district, but since that time the population had very largely increased. Nearly everybody now lived out of town and required increased railway facilities, but the local travelling accommodation was decidedly insufficient. He then said that the proposed railway from the Crystal Palace by way of Ladywell, East London, Cannon Street and Charing Cross, would open up a new route which would be of great advantage to the district and confer an immense boon upon many thousands in London, who could then more easily and cheaply visit the Crystal Palace. It was, he said, nineteen years since the last railway improvement in the neighbourhood when the London, Chatham & Dover Company

❧
Plate 33 - Showing the extensive roof from inside the High Level station in 1921. Plans to extend the branch beyond the station came to nought.
National Railway Museum

Plate 34 - The two 6-wheeled carriages are in one of the two sidings on the Down side of the main line beneath Crystal Palace Parade, probably taken in 1921. The stock to the left is in another set of sidings, predominantly used for carriage stock.   *SECR Society collection*

ran their line through an area at that time still abounding in fields. There followed a motion to submit the proposed railway to Parliament. Mr Wells, in seconding the motion, attributed the number of empty houses in the district to the want of adequate railway service.[3]

The East London, Crystal Palace, and South Eastern Railway Bill was considered by the Standing Order Committee on Tuesday, 6th March 1883. The object of the Bill was to construct a railway from Ladywell station on the mid-Kent branch of the South Eastern Railway Company, to Forest Hill, and thence to a point in the grounds of the Crystal Palace, near the north eastern corner of the orangery. However, the Bill ran into immediate difficulty when the Examiner of Private Bills reported to the Committee that the Bill did not comply with Standing Orders. The Committee then held a consultation in private and came to the conclusion that non compliance with Standing Orders was a sufficient reason to throw out the Bill.[4]

High fares were not the only cause of complaint on the High Level railway. The opening of Upper Sydenham station in 1884 resulted in changes to the timetable. All trains scheduled to stop at Upper Sydenham were timed to leave the High Level station two minutes earlier than usual. However, as the time table alteration was not widely noticed by passengers, many continued to arrive at the terminus only to find that their train had already departed.[5] There were also letters to the local press about the

cab fares from the High Level station. Anyone travelling beyond a one mile radius from the station was charged a cab fare of two shillings.[6] It was therefore suggested that an omnibus service should be started in order to compete with the cabmen.

∗

Amongst other improvements greatly required at Upper Norwood that of a one horse omnibus is readily admitted to be one of the most conspicuous, running from the High Level railway station to somewhere about Beulah Church and another from Low Level station to the far end of Anerly Road. The great difficulty now experienced in all weathers both by young and old, in getting to and from one end of this town to the other on foot, necessitates hundreds of persons daily putting off their pleasures or business, owing to there being no public conveyance but an expensive one to take them to and fro .... The time has arrived when this rapidly increasing place must be for better served with public conveyances than it is at present.[7]

∗

The London, Chatham & Dover Railway failed to respond to any of these complaints, but in 1898 the name of its terminus was changed to Crystal Palace and Upper Norwood in an attempt to attract more passengers from the growing suburbs of Sydenham and Upper Norwood. However, the renaming did little to increase passenger numbers on the High Level line, principally because of competition from the LB&SCR stations at Sydenham, Forest Hill and Honor Oak Park. A brief surge in traffic on the London, Chatham & Dover Railway occurred when the Football Association Cup final between West Bromwich Albion and Aston Villa was held at the new Crystal Palace sports ground in April 1895.

∗

The rival teams, West Bromwich Albion and Aston Villa, proved to be well matched, and the latter had a hard-earned victory by 1 goal to nil …. There was a record attendance, the official returns showing that 42,560 people passed through the various turnstiles. The London Brighton and South Coast and the London Chatham and Dover Railways again proved their capability at dealing with the Sydenham traffic on occasions of emergency, both lines running heavily laden trains speedily, and with reasonable punctuality, to the high and low level stations, so that there was no grumbling to be heard on the part of passengers detained by a tedious journey from town. Between mid-day and half past three o'clock an army of spectators approaching 40,000 strong were safely conveyed from London Bridge, Snow Hill, St Paul's and Victoria, to the Crystal Palace …[8]

∗

By the end of the 19th century the London, Chatham & Dover Railway was deeply unpopular with the travelling public. Repeated feuding with the South Eastern Railway, and failure to adopt joint working procedures with this company, led to severe overcrowding on the suburban lines, and delays were such that nearly 40% of South Eastern and 60% of London, Chatham & Dover trains failed to arrive on time.[9] It was apparent that the amalgamation of the two companies would be beneficial to shareholders and would lead to a more efficient railway system in the south east. Consequently on the 1st January 1899 a working agreement was reached between the two companies, and the South Eastern & Chatham Railway was formed. The South Eastern were to receive 59% of profits and the London,

Chatham & Dover 41%.[10]

When the new guide to the South Eastern & Chatham Railway was published, fares from London to the Crystal Palace High Level station were given as follows:[11]

	First class	Second class	Third class
From London	1s 3d	1s 0d	0s 7d
Return	2s 0d	1s 6d	1s 0d

Return tickets, including admission to the Crystal Palace:

	First class	Second class	Third class
On one shilling days	2s 6d	2s 0d	1s 6d
On two shilling days	4s 6d	4s 0d	3s 6d

Annual season tickets from London: 1st - £12, 2nd - £8

The condition of the amalgamated railways at the time of the working agreement was a cause of great concern to members of the new managing committee. The following story, related by Mr H. Cosmo O. Bonsor, one of the directors, illustrates the difficulties faced by the new company.

∗

The late Lord Burton, who was a very active director and a very active member of the managing committee, … arranged with me, without consulting our officers, that he would borrow from a northern company a locomotive. His idea and mine was that our locomotives were not powerful enough to keep time. The Caledonian Company kindly lent us one of their most improved engines, and it duly arrived. On the following morning the engineer came into my room and said, "I understand that a locomotive has arrived from the north. I cannot possibly allow it to take a train on our system; neither the road nor the bridges will carry it, and if it runs there will be a catastrophe." Immediately afterwards the superintendent of the line came into my room and said, "I understand that a locomotive has arrived from the north which you

❖

Plate 35 - The signal box and sidings at Crystal Palace High Level in 1921 with a train emerging from Paxton tunnel. The early Saxby & Farmer wooden signal box has by now been replaced. Note the carriage sets in the sidings, both straight ahead and on the far side of the approaching train. The coal sidings were to the left, just going out of picture.   *Lambeth Archives*

Plate 36 - Nunhead station in 1920 before remodelling. The Crystal Palace Up line is on the right hand side.   *SECR Society collection*

contemplate running on the line. I am sorry to inform you that there is not a single turn - table which could take it." Well ladies and gentlemen, that locomotive went back to the north but it had done its job, for it brought home to the directors in the most emphatic manner, the work that they had to tackle.

∗

Mr Bonsor also gave details of the work which was eventually carried out on the system '... there were four tunnels which had to be constructed; the whole of the main line road had to be re-laid with heavier rails in place of the light rails which had been in existence since the commencement of the railway, and the ballast, which was shingle, had to be taken out and replaced with Kentish stone. The shingle ballast looked very pretty; it had the appearance of a garden path, and to the uninitiated gave security; but any rainstorm washed it in a way that made the road dangerous. There was another, and almost a bigger job - the reconstruction, rebuilding, and strengthening of the whole of the bridges on the main lines : 588 bridges had to be taken in hand and reconstructed. I hardly like to say at what cost, but it was something over a million sterling.' [12]

The amalgamation of the South Eastern and the London, Chatham & Dover Railways had little immediate effect upon the working of the High Level railway. William Kirtley, the Locomotive Superintendent of the London, Chatham & Dover Railway, resigned at the time of the amalgamation, but motive power on the line continued to be provided by Kirtley-designed Class A 0-4-4Ts, except for the addition of ex-London, Chatham & Dover 'Large Scotchman' Class D 0-4-2Ts which were used

on some passenger trains.[13] Most Chatham carriages were by this time fitted with Westinghouse brakes and Stone's electric lighting, although some were still lit by oil lamps.[14] In 1901 the following letter appeared in the *Sydenham & Penge Gazette* complaining about poorly lit trains: [15]

∗

Sir,

I am, with a few friends, (season ticket holders) petitioning the South Eastern & Chatham Railway to give us a better train, lighted by electric light, for the 1st and 2nd class express from Lordship Lane, Honor Oak, and Crystal Palace to the City, and returning at 4.8, 5.14, and 6.26 from Ludgate - hill. We now have about 8 months of dark evenings to look forward to, and the System of lighting by that particular train is simply abominable in the 20th century. I shall be glad if any season ticket holders who wish for any improvement will kindly send a post card to me with their name and address, and I will add their names to the petition.

I remain,

Yours truly,

P. Howard

Woodland Road, Norwood, S.E.

∗

The petition was subsequently submitted to the South Eastern & Chatham Railway, and the company promised that the train would be taken into the works for modification as soon as possible. Whether electric lighting was fitted in the carriages as a result of the letter is not recorded.

In February 1901 an MP, Mr Frederick John Horniman, donated 15 acres of freehold land, together with an art and natural history museum, to the people of London. The estate was situated close to Lordship Lane station on the South Eastern & Chatham Railway, and consequently it helped to increase passenger traffic on the line when opened to the public. A further increase in traffic was anticipated when in June of the same year the formal opening of Sydenham Wells Park took place. The 17 acres of parkland were close to Upper Sydenham station, thus allowing easy access to the residents of Lewisham and other neighbouring boroughs. In the long term, however, these new facilities generated only a limited increase in traffic on the High Level line.

February 1901 was also the month in which the South Eastern & Chatham Railway Company was taken to the High Court in connection with an alleged assault. Lewis Stroud, a solicitor, claimed that he had been assaulted by a ticket collector at the High Level station whilst leaning his bicycle against a gate at the top of a staircase leading to the platform. The ticket collector apparently tried to close the gate as a train was due to depart, but Stroud leant against the gate to prevent it being shut. A fight then ensued between the ticket collector and Stroud, which resulted in Stroud being thrown down several steps. Several other eye-witnesses of the disturbance gave evidence in support of the plaintiff's case. The ticket collector, however, claimed that he had been struck first and this was confirmed by another railwayman, who alleged that Stroud struck the ticket collector directly he tried to close the gate. Although the jury eventually found in favour of Lewis Stroud, the judge only awarded the sum of one farthing in damages.[16]

The South Eastern & Chatham Railway was also taken to court by the London County Council because of smoke emission from one of its engines. Whilst travelling between Rye Lane and Honor Oak stations an engine drawing a passenger train was seen to emit black smoke for three minutes. The Company did mot contest the case and the Lambeth magistrate imposed a fine of £5 and 23 shillings costs.[17]

As 1901 drew to a close an attempted suicide near to Lordship Lane station was thwarted by the prompt action of a South Eastern & Chatham engine driver. The train was proceeding towards Crystal Palace at about 5pm on a Saturday evening, and whilst travelling between Lordship Lane and Honor Oak stations the driver saw a man come up the railway bank about 12 yards in front of the engine and put his head on the rails. He applied the brake at once and stopped the train at a spot about four feet from the man's head. When asked what he was doing the man replied, 'I want to cut my ----- head off.' The man, Charles Morgan, a grainer of Hindsley Place, Forest Hill, was later charged with trying to commit suicide and was remanded in custody.[18]

The above incident was one a series of accidents and suicide attempts which occurred on the High Level line in the early days of the South Eastern & Chatham Railway. The earliest death occurred at Nunhead station in 1900 when William Cooper, an employee of the railway company, was knocked down by the engine of an up express train. He was on the line when the train approached, and being deaf he did not hear the train whistle.[19] In 1905 Thomas Jackson was driving the engine of a goods train towards the City when, shortly after running through Honor Oak station, he was confronted by a woman who ran from behind a bush onto the line in front of the engine and was knocked down. The lifeless body was placed in the brake van with the assistance of the fireman and guards and was taken to Nunhead station, where a doctor pronounced her dead.[20] When, in 1909, a train arrived at Crystal Palace with a carriage door open, a search along the line revealed a body lying between Lordship Lane station and the tunnel. The body was identified as that of Thomas Taylor, a well known musician and resident of Sydenham, who had been travelling home to Upper Sydenham station. His coat was discovered in the carriage but why he opened the door whilst the train was still in motion was never established.[21] A most dramatic death occurred at Honor Oak station in 1911 when George Hemmings, a political lecturer, was found bleeding from a bullet wound in the station lavatory.

❖

Plate 37 - An ex-LC&DR 'Aeolus' Class 2-4-0T designed by William Martley. Photographed with South Eastern & Chatham Railway markings, the engine is displaying the 'Crystal Palace' headcode.
Kent Libraries and Archives

Plate 38 - Honor Oak station in 1922 just after the departure of a London-bound train. A solitary passenger waits on the down platform; or might she have accompanied the photographer? It was at this station that George Hemmings committed suicide in the station lavatory. He left a suicide note, reproduced below.   *National Railway Museum*

Although propped up on crutches in a standing position, he was dead when found by the Honor Oak booking clerk. A five chamber revolver with one bullet missing was found at his feet. The following suicide note was found on the body:

✳

My dear Marie,
If this reaches you, as I hope it will, the time will have come for you to perform your promise to me. I have reached the limit of my endurance I can bear no more …. Please make my funeral the plainest and cheapest possible. Let who cares follow. There will not be many, but no flowers or invitations. The ring you will find in my waistcoat pocket. Please put it on my finger after death. The locket in the same pocket, please put round my neck. The old Family Bible, with the entry of Aggie's birth in it, I want put in my coffin. I want you to do all this for the cousinly affection there was between your husband and me, and please forgive me for any trouble I may have caused you. The white day shirt in my drawer put on my body, and the gold solitaires I wear put in my cuffs.[22]

✳

In 1902 the continuing need to increase the number of visitors to the Crystal Palace gave rise to two abortive schemes to construct alternative means of transport to Sydenham. The first proposal was for a new light railway to run two and a half miles from Lordship Lane to Crystal Palace, but this was vigorously opposed by the London County Council, the South Eastern & Chatham Railway Company, the Estates Governors of Dulwich College and various local authorities. The Crystal Palace Light Railways and Tramways Company was therefore forced to withdraw its application for an order authorising the construction work.[23] The second scheme was to re-appear in various forms throughout the life of the High Level railway. It was suggested that a tube railway should be constructed to the Crystal Palace, and the Chairman of the Crystal Palace scheme, Mr Schenk, offered to find the sum of £1 million pounds towards the construction if the appropriate Act was passed. However, when a Committee of the House of Lords considered this underground railway scheme it was decided not to proceed.[24] The idea, however, was obviously not abandoned, for in 1909 in a speech made to the Sydenham, Forest Hill and District Chamber of Commerce, Mr E. L. Bingham, the secretary, made the following comment:

✳

In the early part of last year you were informed that a company had been formed for the purpose of obtaining Parliamentary powers to construct a tube railway from the City to the Crystal Palace, via Forest Hill and Sydenham. Nothing has yet been done, but judging from the remarks made by the Chairman of the Crystal Palace Company at their recent annual meeting, I should imagine that it is not merely a castle in the air, but that before long something definite will be done in the matter.[25]

*

The name to be given to the new tube line was reported as 'The Sydenham, Victoria, and West-end Electric Tube Railway'.[26] However, nothing further was heard of the scheme until June 1913 when the Lord Mayor, speaking at a banquet of the Royal Institute of British Architects, observed that the Crystal Palace was every minute becoming nearer to London by a tube, which he knew - he was able to speak now on good authority - would be extended to the Crystal Palace in the near future.[27] In November of the same year the Lord Mayor wrote to the Mayor of Camberwell stating that:

*

I have had an interview with a representative of the Underground Railways of London, who are prepared to continue the Tube Railway from the Elephant and Castle to Camberwell Green, Champion Hill, Dulwich, Lordship Lane, Sydenham Hill Road, West Hill, and under the Crystal Palace, Norwood end.

*

The scheme was sufficiently well advanced for the press to point out that:

*

So favourably do the Underground authorities consider the proposal that already a tentative route and the number of stations necessary have been mapped out, and according to present plans the stations would be Camberwell Green,

Champion Hill, Dulwich, Lordship Lane, Sydenham Hill Road, West Hill, Crystal Palace (Norwood side).[28]

*

It all sounded extremely promising but the following year saw the commencement of the Great War, and consequently nothing further was heard of the proposal for the new tube line.

When royal visits to the Crystal Palace occurred the arrival at the High Level station was invariably marked by a ceremonial procedure on the station platform. In 1902 the Prince and Princess of Wales paid a visit in order to attend the London Diocesan Juvenile Branch of the Church of England Temperance Society. They left Victoria station by a special train and arrived at the High Level station at 1.30pm. The Prince and Princess were met on the platform by the Bishop of London, the Bishop of Kensington, the Rev. H. Russell Wakefield, Mr Ernest Schenk (chairman of the Crystal Palace Company), Captain the Hon. Arthur Somerset and Mr Henry Gillman - the manager of the Palace. A guard of honour, consisting of a detachment of the Church Lads' Brigade under Major Hamilton, was also drawn up on the platform. The royal visitors were then conducted from the station to the concert room in the Palace.[29]

The Shah of Persia also visited the Palace in 1902 in order to view the Co-operative Flower Show. The press reported his arrival thus:

*

His Imperial Majesty, attended by his suite, and accompanied by Prince Arthur of Connaught, the Earl of Kintore, Colonel the Hon. H. C. Legge, Sir A. Hardinge

Plate 39 - A postcard of Cox's Walk footbridge, near Lordship Lane station, in either LC&DR or SE&CR days.   *Lens of Sutton Association*

The Bridge, Cox's Walk, Dulwich.

Plate 40 - Another postcard, this time of Lordship Lane station from Cox's Walk footbridge in the LC&DR or SE&CR era showing a steam-hauled train bound for Crystal Palace. The short siding was removed during electrification work in 1925.   *Lens of Sutton Association*

and Colonel Chenevix Trench, reached the High Level station at the Crystal Palace by a special train from Windsor at 7.30pm. A guard of honour was mounted by the 4th V.B. Royal West Surrey Regiment. The illustrious visitor was received by Mr Schenk (chairman) and other directors of the Crystal Palace Company, the general manager Mr Henry Gilman, the band of the 10th (Prince of Wales's Own) Royal Hussars playing the Persian National Anthem.[30]

*

These occasions brought large numbers of visitors, and much needed revenue, to the Crystal Palace and the railway companies. In particular the 'Festival of Empire and Imperial Exhibition', which was held between March and October 1911, proved to be extremely popular with the public. To cope with demand for this event the South Eastern & Chatham Railway cut the journey time of its trains from Victoria to the Palace to 15 minutes. This necessitated an average speed of 39 mph, on a difficult run, with tare loads around 120 tons. When, on 30th June 1911, a one-day event for school children took place during the festival it was necessary for the railway company to run 47 special trains to accommodate the traffic. Consequently 90 additional staff were employed at Crystal Palace and 61 of the 98 regular trains had to be cancelled to allow the working of the specials.[31] A total of 100,000 London schoolchildren attended the event, of which 32,000 were handled at the High Level station.[32]

On 1st January 1903 both the London, Brighton & South Coast Railway and the South Eastern & Chatham Railway

announced the suspension of all through bookings which included admission to the Crystal Palace. The railway companies claimed that this action was taken because of a notice which had been received from the Crystal Palace Company. However, this met with an angry rebuttal from Mr Schenk, the chairman of that company, who stated that '... the responsibility for the alteration in the arrangements rests absolutely with the railway companies .... my Company has done its utmost to persuade them to continue those arrangements.'

He was also displeased with the proposal of the railway companies to take a larger share of the 1s 6d third class tickets.

*

Our effort to persuade the railway companies to reconsider their decision ended in an interview between our joint boards, but we were met by a stolid refusal ...' [33]

*

The dispute was, however, quickly resolved for on 31st January 1903 both railway companies agreed to re-instate the bookings at the same fares as were in force prior to 1st January 1903. However, no concession was made on the price of third class fares, which were increased from 1s 6d to 1s 9d.[34] This short-lived dispute brought to a head the bad feeling which existed between the railway companies and the Crystal Palace company. Mr Schenk, the Crystal Palace chairman, continued to berate the railway companies in the local press.

*

The attitude of the railway companies towards the Crystal Palace has long been an unfriendly one .... Mr J Staats Forbes (Chairman of the LCDR) stated twenty years ago, and has always maintained, that the Crystal Palace could never succeed, and that the sooner its 200 acres were built over the better. The same view has been expressed by three out of four general managers of the two railway companies who have held office within the last four years. Any attempt to secure for the Palace additional means of access, even much needed local tramways, is strenuously opposed by the companies, and regarded by them as an unfriendly act, calling for reprisals.[35]

＊

Both the South Eastern & Chatham and the London, Brighton & South Coast Railway companies did, however, eventually make a concession to season ticket holders. In 1906 it was agreed that season ticket holders on either of the two lines could purchase a joint season ticket which would allow them to use both of the lines between London and the Crystal Palace. The additional cost of this ticket was set at £4 per annum. This concession was brought about by a petition raised by two Upper Norwood residents. However, it received a lukewarm reaction from other season ticket holders who considered that £4 per annum for third class, £12 for second class and £16 for first class, was out of proportion to the value of the additional facilities.[36]

Of the two companies the London, Brighton & South Coast Railway appeared to offer cheaper return fares to London, as the writer of the following letter pointed out:

＊

Sir,
It is difficult to understand the antiquated methods of the Chatham and Dover Railway (SECR). Why do they allow the London Brighton and South Coast Railway to get nearly all the passenger traffic between the Crystal Palace and London? Naturally, when one can travel after 11am, in a comfortable carriage and for one half the price by the Brighton Line, everyone avoids the Chatham and Dover (SECR).
At Lordship Lane the tram runs right past the door of the station, and yet this antediluvian line does not make the slightest effort to meet the competition to Victoria. If people could get a cheap return ticket from Crystal Palace (High Level) or Lordship Lane to the Elephant and Castle, many would prefer that route for getting to Trafalgar Square and Piccadilly, instead of travelling by the Brighton line to London Bridge and thence to the Elephant by the ill ventilated City and South London Tube.
It really makes one hope the Government will some day take over the railways, they are so necessary nowadays that they ought to be run for the benefit of the community even although it be at a loss.[37]

＊

TEMPORARY CLOSURE

In 1911 the Crystal Palace, its popularity having steadily declined, became insolvent and as a consequence the Palace and its grounds were put up for auction. Lord Plymouth initially purchased the property, but following a successful fundraising campaign the Crystal Palace eventually passed into public ownership.

The year 1911 was also the year that railway workers went on strike to obtain recognition of their trade union, a 72-hour week and a weekly wage of 27 shillings.[38] The strike did not last long, but whilst in progress it proved to be advantageous to London County Council trams, which by this time were operating in the Sydenham area and were providing serious competition for the railway companies. Trams were cheap and frequent and consequently they took business away from the railways. When, as a result of the strike, workmen's tickets were suspended and it was announced that Cannon Street station was closed, there was an early morning rush for the London County Council tramcars and every Southwark Bridge and Victoria tram went away overloaded.[39]

It is ironic that the industrial unrest of 1911 occurred just three years before the railway companies and their employees were called upon to work together to achieve maximum efficiency in the interests of the country during the Great War. In April 1914 the last Cup Final to be played at the Crystal Palace brought large crowds to Sydenham. This was the last event to be held at the Palace before war brought about its closure. However, the building continued to be used, as it was then taken over and became a training depot for Royal Navy personnel.[40]

In August 1914 the war with Germany began, and as a consequence the Government assumed control over the railways. The South Eastern & Chatham, being the nearest railway to the Channel, was immediately called upon to convey troops, ammunition and stores, to the ports, and SE&CR steamers were then utilised to transport the men and equipment abroad. Austerity measures were necessary and consequently '... the Wainwright livery was abandoned for an unlined lead grey for locomotives and brown for coaches. Stations were closed, never to re-open, and intensive services and borrowed locomotives were used to maintain the flow of men and materials to the front.'[41]

Train services on the High Level line continued as normal until January 1915, when the South Eastern & Chatham announced cuts in their suburban services.

❀

Plate 41 above - A handsome platform lamp at Upper Sydenham in SE&CR days. Note that the rear facet is opaque. These lamps were in use at the intermediate stations on the branch. *Lens of Sutton Association*

*

The Management Committee regret the inconvenience to the travelling public, and hope that no further restrictions may be necessary. So soon as it is possible the cancelled services will be restored.[42]

*

As a result of this, the number of trains to the Crystal Palace from the City were firstly reduced and then stopped altogether on 1st April 1916.[43] The Board of Trade then put forward a proposal that the line should be completely closed. However, this was vigorously opposed by season ticket holders and regular users. In December 1916 a meeting was held at the Caxton Hall to protest about the proposed closure of the line:

*

Mr Albert E. Cave, who presided, said that over 100 letters had been received expressing agreement with the protest. He moved a resolution declaring that the closing would produce widespread hardship and inconvenience in the districts affected, and that the meeting suggested to the Board of Trade as alternatives to the proposal :-

A service limited to the morning and evening for business people going to the City and West End; and a motor train running in connection with the service from the City and West End to Nunhead. By adoption of the alternatives a large amount of labour and rolling stock could be released for other purposes .... the meeting also adopted as a third suggestion that a service should be run as far as Lordship Lane.' [44]

*

Despite the fact that a committee was formed to negotiate with the Board of Trade and the South Eastern & Chatham Railway, none of the objectives set out at the meeting were achieved. On 1st January 1917 passenger services on the Nunhead and Crystal Palace branch were suspended, leaving only coal trains to run on the line as required.

The suspension of passenger services led to the closure of the High Level station, and the station master, Mr Walter Chave, was therefore forced to move from the area. He had previously worked at the station from 1876 to 1886 when it was busy and profitable due to the prosperity of the Crystal Palace. He returned to the High Level station after 21 years absence and worked an additional nine years until 1916. When interviewed by the press he spoke regretfully of the prospect of leaving Norwood, but said that from a traffic point of view the condition of things was very different to when he was there previously.[45]

All of the railway companies at this time restricted their passenger services to allow the transportation of materials for the war. The public were also advised that it was unpatriotic to travel for pleasure.

*

These are abnormal times, and the sooner the conditions in which we are living are realised the less the inconvenience and worry suffered by individuals, and the greater the energy which can be thrown into the effort to bring the

Plate 42 - Upper Sydenham station in SE&CR days looking towards Crescent Wood tunnel and Lordship Lane. Note the Down starter is positioned on the Up side to facilitate sighting by the train crew. The quantity of ivy adorning the box, which is similar in style to the original one at the High Level station, may be questionable as it is likely to inhibit visibility from the box.   *Lens of Sutton Association*

war to its due conclusion as speedily as possible ... The warning that has been issued, stating that the railway companies cannot undertake to convey passengers to any particular destination, has been made absolutely essential by existing conditions, and on the principle that to be forewarned is to be forearmed, the public will be wise if they take serious notice of it ... To put it bluntly, we do not desire passenger traffic.[46]

*

On the same day as passenger services were suspended on the High Level line, the Railway Executive Committee introduced draconian regulations to deter the public from travelling:

*

Train journeys, so long as the limitations remain in force, will be expensive and attended by a certain amount of inconvenience, but the measures taken by the Railway Executive Committee are regarded as essential to enable the companies to cope with imperative war demands at home and in France. The principal changes may be summarized under the following heads :-

Ordinary fares are increased by 50%. The only exceptions are workmen's, season, traders', and zone tickets. Every other form of cheap ticket is abolished.

About 400 trains have been withdrawn from the time-tables and others will take longer on their journeys.

Many stations are temporarily closed.

The reservations of seats or compartments and the provision of saloons are discontinued.

The running of restaurant and sleeping cars is further curtailed.

Slip coaches are withdrawn.

Motor-cars or carriages will not be carried on passenger trains.

Luggage is restricted to 100lb for each passenger.

All season tickets must be shown or ordinary fare paid.[47]

*

When the High Level line closed on 1st January 1917 passengers who held unexpired season tickets were allowed to use them on the London, Brighton & South Coast Railway. Consequently, when the line reopened on 1st March 1919, passengers who held season tickets which had been taken out with the London, Brighton & South Coast Railway assumed that they would be able to use the tickets on the South Eastern & Chatham Railway. It was even suggested that all classes of tickets should be permanently interchangeable in order to relieve the overcrowding which was occurring on the London, Brighton &

South Coast line from Crystal Palace. However, passengers were to be disappointed, for when the issue was raised with the South Eastern & Chatham Railway, the Secretary stated that unexpired season tickets on the London, Brighton & South Coast Railway could not be used on the South Eastern & Chatham.[48]

Although the High Level line reopened on the 1st March 1919 the service to Victoria was permanently abandoned. It was therefore only possible to use the South Eastern & Chatham to travel to the City, although residents in the Sydenham area could utilise the services of the London, Brighton & South Coast Railway to reach Victoria.[49] The abandonment of the Victoria service on the South Eastern & Chatham took place at the same time as renewed discussions were held concerning the possible construction of a tube line to the Crystal Palace. In July 1919 a meeting of the Select Committee of the House of Commons was held to inquire into London's transport problems. When asked to consider whether new tubes were contemplated in South London, Mr Blain, operating manager of the London traffic group said '... he was hopeful that they might be able to come to an arrangement with the SE&CR so that they might be able to utilise their lines. They had also considered several plans for the extension of the tube system in South London. At present the cost was very heavy, and they would prefer to see some such arrangement as existed in North London with the railway companies. One scheme they had in mind was a line by way of Dulwich right up to the Crystal Palace.'[50]

The tube line from Dulwich to the Crystal Palace did not materialise, but the scheme continued to be discussed throughout the life of the High Level line.

All of the railways gave exemplary service during the Great War, but the South Eastern & Chatham Railway had a particularly fine record of war service. The following letter was sent to Cosmo Bonsor, Chairman of the South Eastern & Chatham Managing Committee, by Sir Douglas Haig, the Commander in Chief of the British Army in France:

*

The Army in France owes much to all connected with the control of our railway companies in the United Kingdom, and indeed in the Empire. They have at all times shown the greatest willingness to help us in every possible way in their power. Track has been torn up to give us rails; engines, trucks, men, capable engineers, operations staff, &c., all have been sent abroad to us, regardless of their own special needs and demands of the people at home, and without a moment's hesitation.

But we have been more closely associated with the South Eastern and Chatham Railway than any other. The bulk of our ammunition and stores required for the maintenance of our armies, as well as several millions of men as reinforcements and on leave, have passed over their system. Their sphere of duty, too, has been nearest to the shores of France and Belgium, and consequently more open to hostile attacks by air and fears of invasion by sea. Undisturbed by any alarms the traffic for the Armies in France has never ceased to flow. This reflects the greatest credit on all concerned with the Company.[51]

*

Plate 43 - The tudor style chimneys are in evidence at Lordship Lane station. Design considerations were heavily influenced by the demands of the Governors of the Estate of Alleyn's College of God's Gift, through whose land the line was built. The station building afforded access to the Down platform at first floor level.

Lens of Sutton Association

Pictorial Survey

Lordship Lane

Upper Sydenham

(Below) Plate 44 - Cox's Walk footbridge No.448 with Lordship Lane station visible in the distance, 17th September 1954.

Denis Cullum

(Left) Plate 45 - 4-SUB No.4485 leaving Lordship Lane en-route to Crystal Palace High Level. Note the more modern carriage inserted into the original three-car set.

Mike Morant

Plate 46 - 4-SUB unit No.4720 working the 5.04pm Blackfriars-Crystal Palace coasts to a halt.

Denis Cullum at Lordship Lane, 17th September 1954

Plate 47 - The two platforms and signal box. Note the transition from wooden platforms to a hard surface, as well as a narrowing of the platforms, following extensions to accommodate longer trains. Cox's Walk footbridge is visible just as the lines curve out of sight.

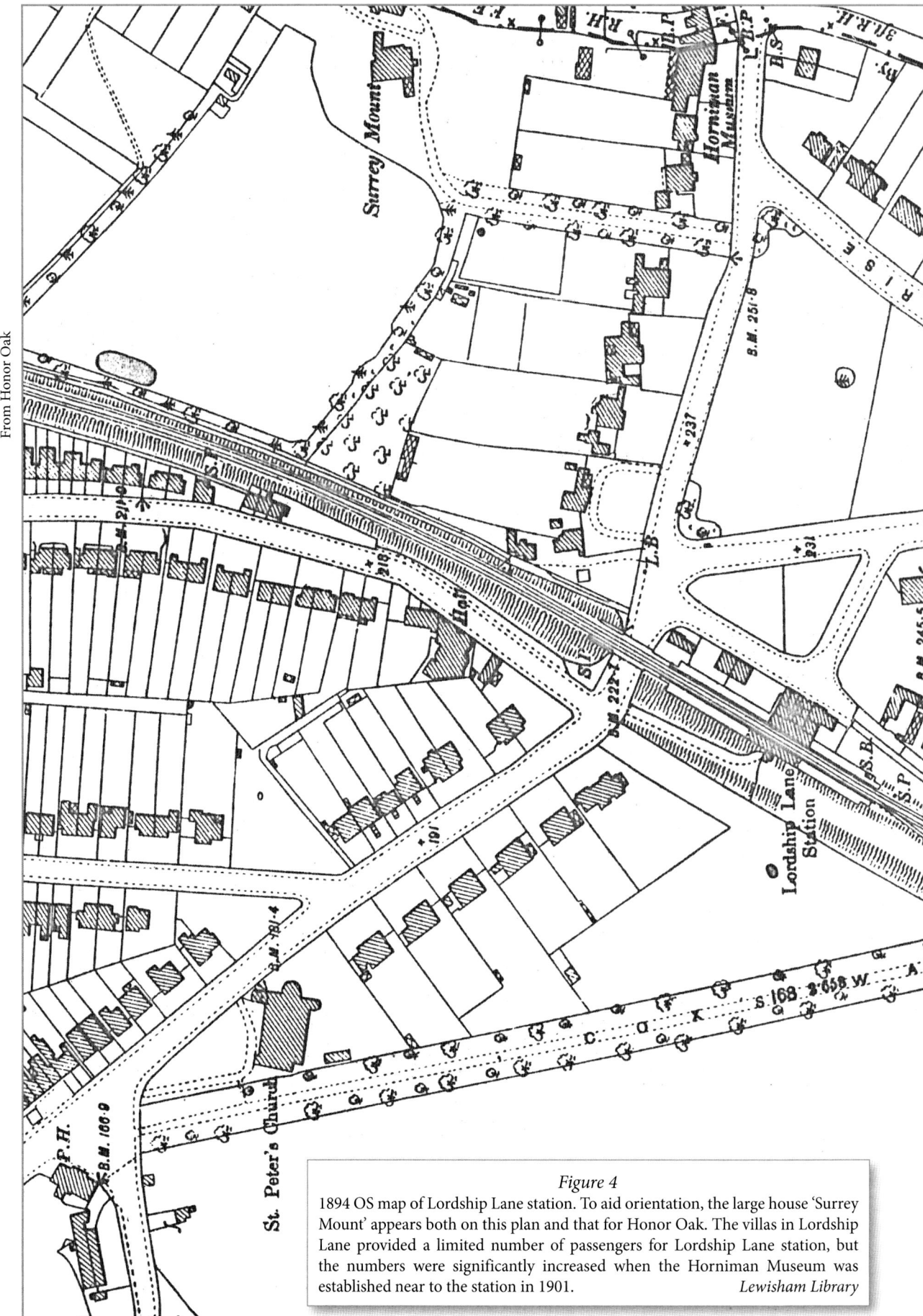

Figure 4
1894 OS map of Lordship Lane station. To aid orientation, the large house 'Surrey Mount' appears both on this plan and that for Honor Oak. The villas in Lordship Lane provided a limited number of passengers for Lordship Lane station, but the numbers were significantly increased when the Horniman Museum was established near to the station in 1901.   *Lewisham Library*

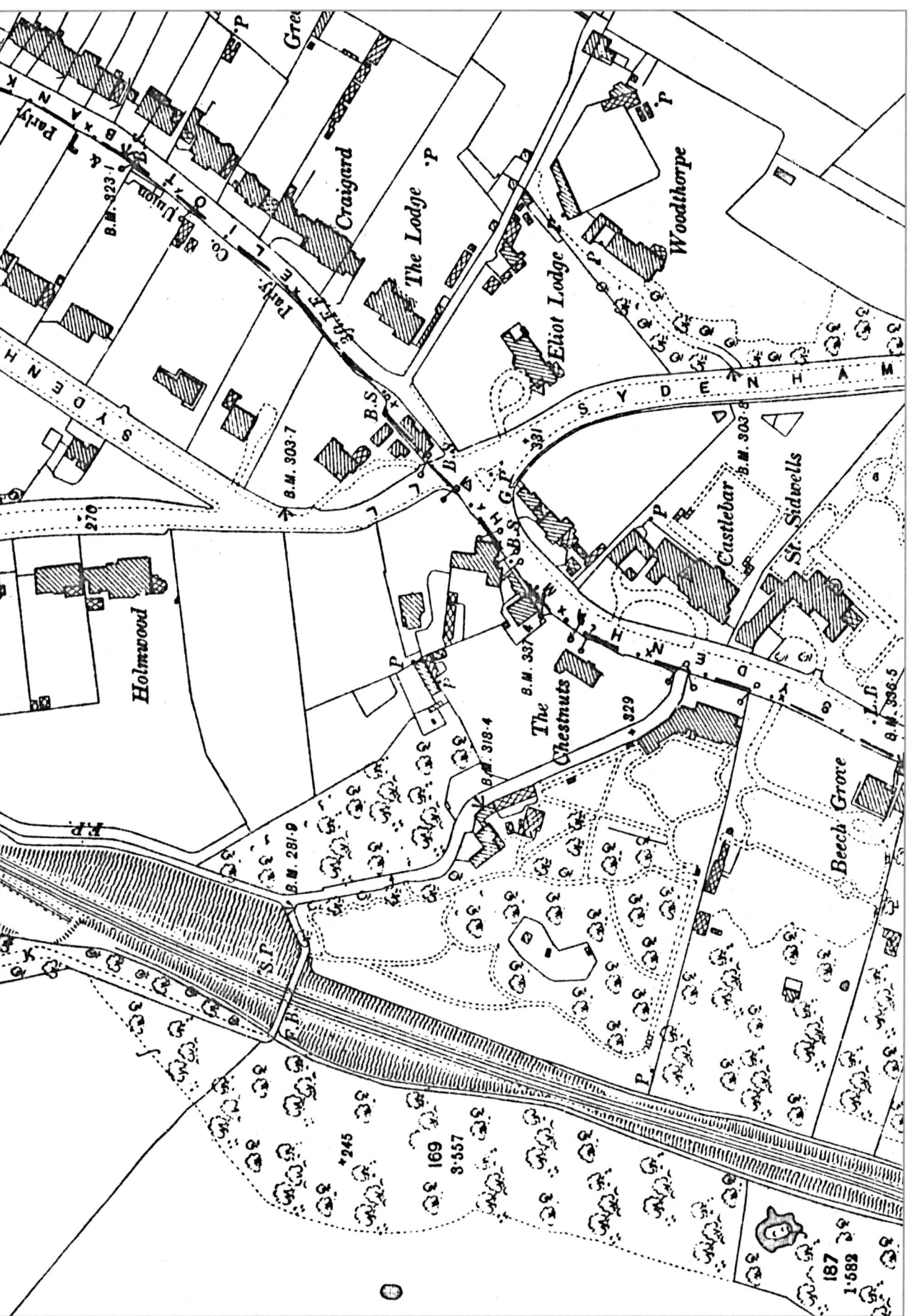

To Upper
Sydenham

Plate 48 - A 1950s view of the platform side of the main station building at Lordship Lane. Wartime bombing resulted in the removal of the canopies on both platforms.   *Lens of Sutton Association*

Plate 49 - The earth slip which occurred at Upper Sydenham in 1947 demolished a waiting shelter on the Up platform. The area affected by the slip is quite evident in this view. In most of these pictures, passengers are conspicuous by their absence!   *Lens of Sutton Association*

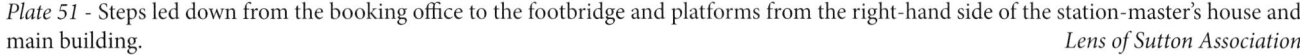

Plate 50 - The unprepossessing entrance to Upper Sydenham station in Wells Road shortly after closure in September 1954. The station sign is still carrying the Southern Electric title, although the timetable boards on the fence proclaim British Railways. *Lens of Sutton Association*

Plate 51 - Steps led down from the booking office to the footbridge and platforms from the right-hand side of the station-master's house and main building. *Lens of Sutton Association*

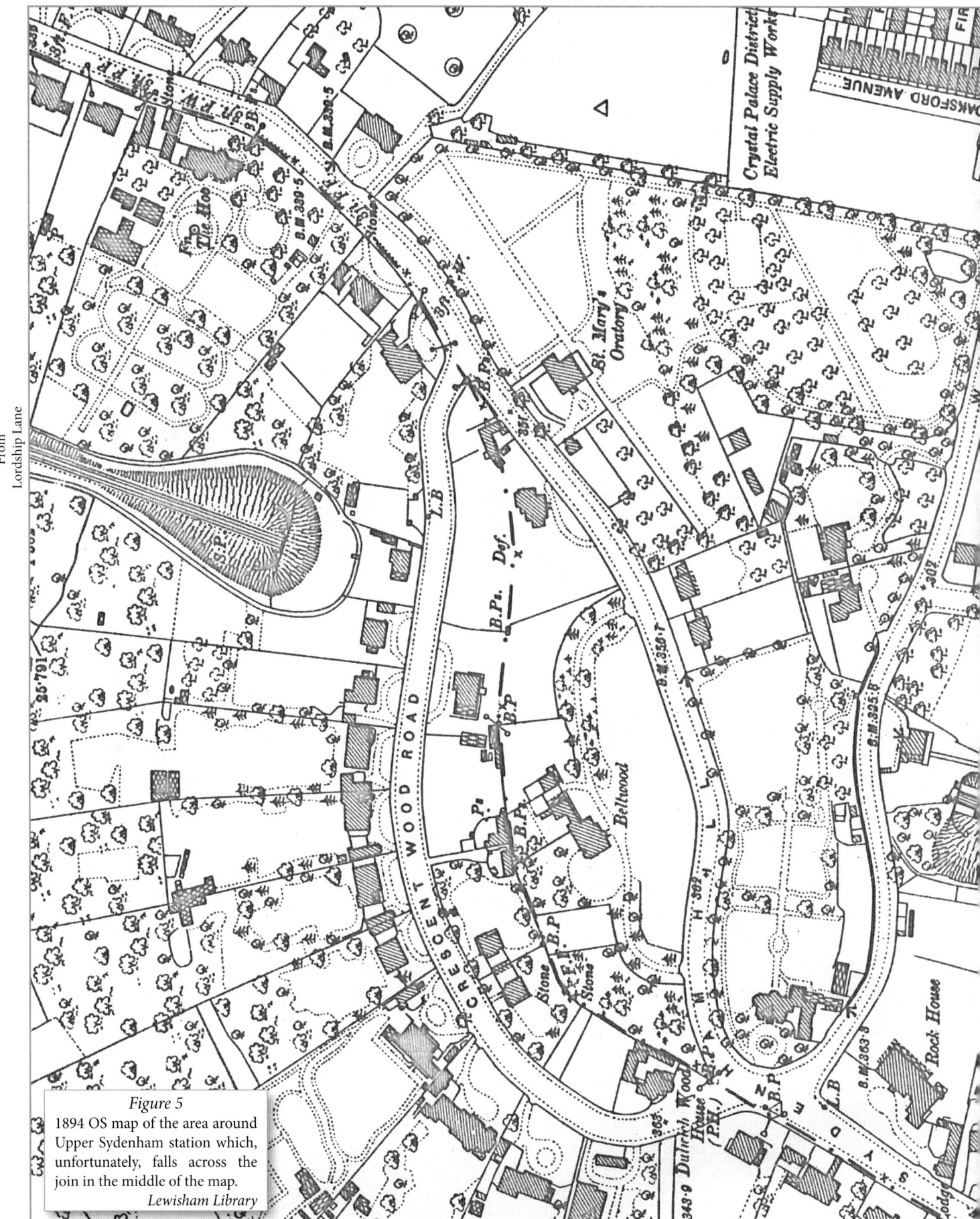

Figure 5
1894 OS map of the area around Upper Sydenham station which, unfortunately, falls across the join in the middle of the map.
Lewisham Library

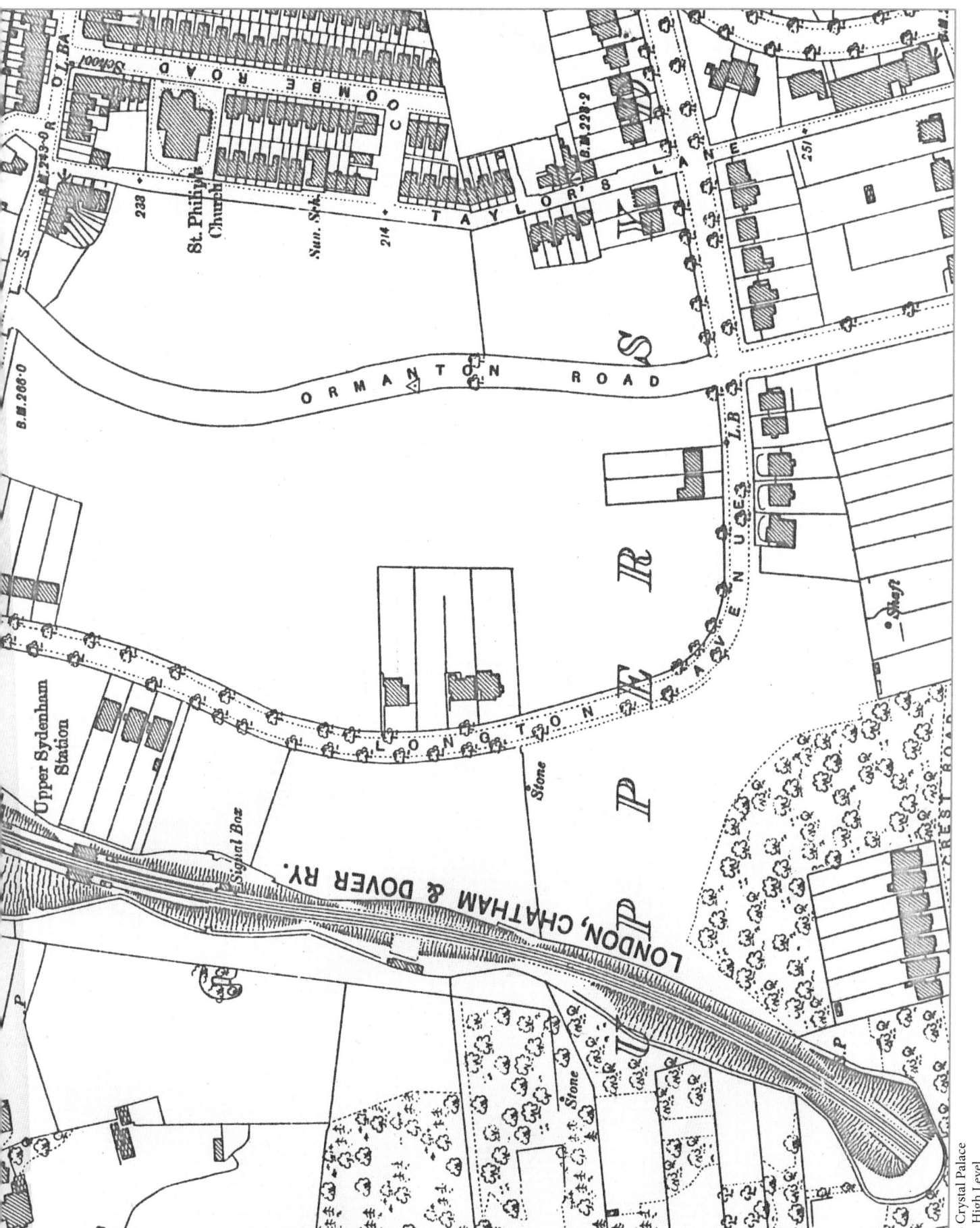

To Crystal Palace
High Level

Plate 52 - Upper Sydenham station in 1922, looking into Crescent Wood tunnel. The large ivy-covered building on the hill is the stationmaster's house, which also houses the booking office and station offices; there is an awning visible at the left-hand edge of the house, probably protecting the booking office window. The signals by the tunnel mouth are barely visible, although there does appear to be a white-painted portion of the tunnel mouth brickwork to aid sighting. *National Railway Museum*

Plate 53 - The stationmaster's house is now boarded-up and with broken windows but is no longer ivy covered. The entrance was in Wells Road, above the cutting, and steps led down from the house to the station platforms; the railings are easily visible. *National Railway Museum*

Plate 54 - North portal of Crescent Wood tunnel, 17th September 1954. A catch point, which is marked on the plan shown in *Figure 3,* is just visible this side of the distant signal, the ruling gradient being 1 in 78. There is plenty of detail on view for the modeller; the small p-way hut, the lineside cable run and the telegraph pole, just for starters. The diamond-shaped board is probably an indicator of the catch-point's position.
Denis Cullum

Plate 55 - A modeller's view of the Upper Sydenham Down platform waiting shelter. Note the protective boards either side of the conductor rail as the line is crossed by the walk-way. 18th October 1950.
Lens of Sutton Association

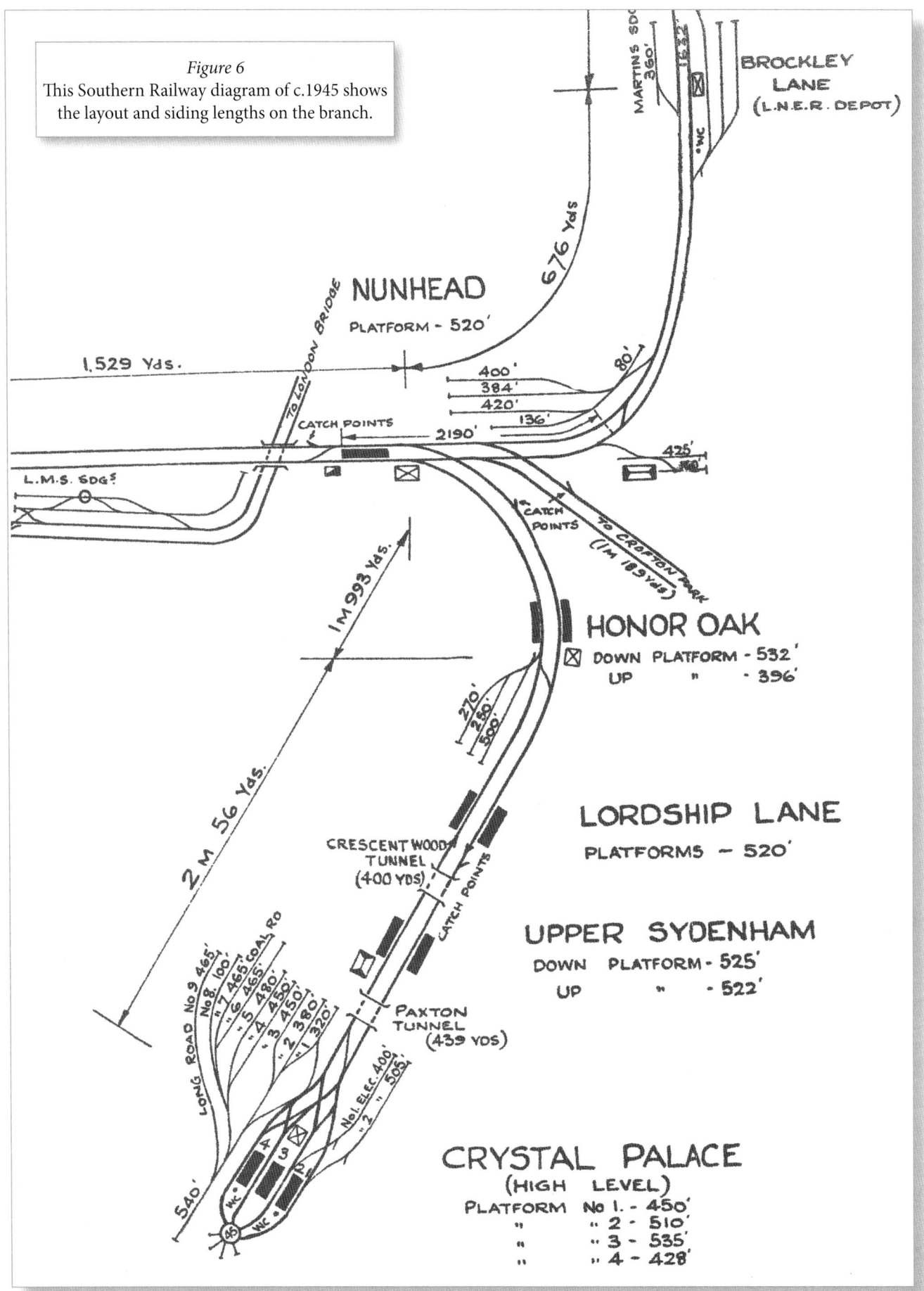

Figure 6
This Southern Railway diagram of c.1945 shows
the layout and siding lengths on the branch.

❧ *Chapter Five* ❧

THE SOUTHERN RAILWAY

The Crystal Palace did not re-open immediately after World War I. After its temporary use as a training depot maintenance work needed to be carried out, and therefore it was not until June 1920 that the official re-opening was undertaken by King George V. The Palace regained much of its popularity by staging exhibitions, firework displays, brass band contests and dirt track racing events.[1] Huge crowds visited the Palace on these occasions, and most travelled by train, utilising both the South Eastern & Chatham and the London, Brighton & South Coast Railways.

In August 1920 the General Manager of the Crystal Palace, Mr Henry J. Buckland, faced a protest from exhibitors at the Palace concerning the poor transportation facilities offered by the two railway companies:

*

The railway companies could have helped a great deal by the institution of quick and cheap services of trains from various parts of the country, but absolutely nothing appears to have been done in this matter.

*

Friction between the Crystal Palace Company and the South Eastern & Chatham and London, Brighton & South Coast Railways had existed for many years, chiefly because of the refusal of the railway companies to provide cheaper services. This was pointed out by the General Manager of the Palace when he replied at length in the local press to the disgruntled exhibitors:

*

The railway facilities are admittedly not of the best, but this is no fault of the Palace management who months ago received the promise of the two railway companies serving the district that more frequent and better facilities would be given. The motor omnibus service has helped considerably.[2]

*

Buses and trams were steadily taking passengers away from the railways, and in 1921 a new competitor appeared on the scene, the motor char-a-banc. These vehicles offered cheap trips to the coast and were operated between Easter and October. The firm of 'Passengers Motor Services', which was based in Croydon, ran trips to Eastbourne and Brighton, but also ran half-day trips to Windsor. During the 1921 season this firm carried between thirty and forty thousand people. However, the managing director of the firm, Mr J. B. Skyrme, was quick to point out that motoring by char-a-banc would not be a competitor with railways:

*

The conditions are wholly against this. The railways can take a practically unlimited number of people with the same engine, and the journey is necessarily quicker. Obviously the accommodation by motor char-a-banc must, on the other hand, be limited.[3]

*

However, events held at the Crystal Palace continued to provide pleasure traffic for the South Eastern & Chatham. In October 1922 it was announced that a great carnival, to include a fancy dress dance and parade, would be held in the centre transept of the Crystal Palace. This event enabled the South Eastern & Chatham to run special trains up to midnight from the High Level station, thereby enabling passengers to connect with the last trains on the District and Bakerloo Railways. The London, Brighton & South Coast Railway also ran trains

❧

Plate 56 - A 1930s view of Cox's Walk footbridge where Camille Pissarro set up his easel to paint Lordship Lane station.

Postcard from Card House

from the Low Level station for the event, and these stopped at all stations to New Cross and Victoria up to 12.15am. The 11.33pm also stopped at Norwood Junction for Sutton and other stations.[4]

When Mr W. J. Wood, the station master at the High Level station, promoted a concert to be held at the Parish Church Hall, Ladywell Road, in aid of the Railway Servants' Orphanage, Derby, the South Eastern & Chatham Railway received favourable publicity in the local press. This charitable institution looked after the orphans of railwaymen, and was offering to admit two children of any man killed in the Great War. Over a period of thirty-five years the sum of £4,533 had been raised for the orphanage by employees, and Mr Wood appealed for further subscriptions from residents in the neighbourhood.[5] Mr Wood was a popular station master and two years later, when his daughter was married at St Stephen's, South Dulwich, a comprehensive report of the wedding also appeared in the local press. Mr Wood and his wife apparently lived on the station premises, for it was reported that '... the reception was held at the home of the bride's parents at the High Level station.'[6]

However, not all employees of the South Eastern & Chatham were trustworthy. In December 1922 John Robert Holloway, an employee of the railway company, appeared at Lambeth Police Court to answer a charge of theft. Whilst working at Lordship Lane station he had stolen £31 1s 5d, and for this he was fined the sum of £20. He was also required to repay the stolen money.[7]

By 1923 the South Eastern & Chatham Railway had completed plans for the complete electrification of their lines. Under the Trade Facilities Act the company had made arrangements which enabled the capital for the scheme to be provided under a Government guarantee as to both principal and interest. Three supply companies had tendered for the contract to electrify the lines, and the London Electric Supply Corporation had been awarded the contract.[8] However, there were delays in the implementation of the scheme and 1923 was also the year in which the merging of the railway companies into four major groups was proposed. Consequently the South Eastern

& Chatham Railway did not proceed with the electrification scheme but instead the company handed the plans over to the newly formed Southern Railway.[9]

The amalgamation combined all of the railways in Britain into four groups. In this way 120 companies were reduced to four, the Great Western Railway, the London, Midland & Scottish Railway, the London & North Eastern Railway and the Southern Railway. The Southern Railway, which was the smallest of the four groups, was comprised of the South Eastern & Chatham, the London & South Western and the London, Brighton & South Coast Railways.[10] The new groupings offered a number of advantages; better and more varied services, faster goods traffic, elimination of superfluous services, a reduction of overlapping, the standardisation of all engines, coaches, trucks, permanent way and equipment generally.[11]

The directors of the Southern Railway Company immediately announced that the sum of £8,000,000 would be allocated for new works. From this sum £5,250,000 was to be spent on electrification, and the target date for the completion of the electrification programme was to be the end of 1925. In order to operate the electrified railway system, orders were placed in the railway company's own workshops for the reconstruction of locomotives, carriages and wagons, and with British firms for the construction of motor coaches. Orders were also placed for 400,00 tons of steel rails and fish plates. The line to Crystal Palace via Nunhead and Honor Oak was included in the list of lines from Victoria to be electrified.[12]

The Southern Railway also announced that the terminus at Crystal Palace would be renamed Crystal Palace High Level, presumably to increase its importance and to attract more passengers. The High Level and Low Level stations were now a part of the same company, so season ticket holders were also

❋

Plate 57 - The lamp on the right seems to dominate this photograph of Nunhead in 1921, just before the station was to become part of the Southern Railway. Within about four years the station was remodelled as a single island platform, opening as such on 3rd May 1925.

National Railway Museum

Plate 58 - Lordship Lane in 1922. The crossover was probably removed as part of the electrification programme in 1925 and it is quite likely that the siding visible in *Plate 40* was also removed at that time. Note the lamps, typical of the intermediate stations. *National Railway Museum*

granted a concession denied them during the days of the South Eastern & Chatham. Season ticket holders from the Crystal Palace High Level station were able to use their seasons to and from the Low Level station on Sundays when the High Level station was closed.[13]

It was hoped that electrification would provide faster and more frequent trains to and from the City, and to other stations in the Greater London area. The local press was particularly enthusiastic:

∗

A material shortening of the time occupied in a journey to London should result in the company recovering much of the traffic that was lost with the coming of the electric trams and the development of the bus services .... The full use of the railway for suburban traffic must result in some alleviation of the congestion on the roads which is reaching a perilous point and causing grave anxiety to the Metropolitan Traffic Authorities.[14]

∗

The High Level line was one of the first to be converted to suburban third-rail electrification. The scheme involved the lengthening of the platforms at Honor Oak and Lordship Lane and closure of signal boxes at Nunhead Bank, Lordship Lane and Upper Sydenham.[15] The London Electric Supply Corporation transmitted alternating current at 11,000 volts from a switch room at Lewisham, through lineside cables, to 19 rotary substations where it was converted to 660 volts direct current and fed into the conductor rails. At Upper Sydenham it

was necessary to construct a substation which served both the Crystal Palace branch and the main line. This was achieved by utilising a ventilation shaft to run cables into the Penge tunnel which ran below the High Level line.[16] This tunnel, which was a mile and a quarter in length, had the reputation of being one of the most foul on the whole of the Southern Railway system. It was maintained by a gang of platelayers which included Charles Thomas Symonds, aged 68, who had spent 49 years on night work in the tunnel without ever having had a days illness. Symonds attributed his health to the sulphur fumes in the tunnel caused by between 40 to 55 trains which passed through during his eight hour shift.[17]

In March 1925 Sir Herbert Walker, the General Manager, visited both the Brighton and Ashford works of the Southern Railway in order to check on the progress being made on electrification work. He was accompanied by other members of the Southern Board and representatives of the press. After inspecting the construction and assembly of new rolling stock, Sir Herbert Walker addressed the party and pointed out that electrification work was not being undertaken in order to economise, as the whole idea of electrification was to increase traffic. The more trains that they could run into their terminals, the greater was the capacity of the line. He anticipated that with electrified lines they could run two and a half trains for every one train run now. These increased facilities would have a most beneficial effect on the millions of travellers who used the Southern Railway, besides being of material benefit to their districts.[18]

Training for the staff who would operate the electric services from Nunhead to the Crystal Palace High Level station commenced on 1st April 1925.[19] On Monday, 8th June 1925 an electric train ran for the first time on the High Level line. This trial run was reported in the press in the following manner:

*

Something quite new in the annals of our local railways occurred on Monday, when for the first time an electric train ran over the S. E. section of the Southern Railway from Wells Road (Upper Sydenham) station, to Ravensbourne, via Catford, and back to St Paul's .... it is gratifying to know that some part of Sydenham and Forest Hill is now to be served by electric trains, and that the stations include Upper Sydenham, Lordship Lane, Honor Oak, Crofton Park, and Nunhead. The new service will probably be inaugurated on July 12th.

Monday's test seems to have been very satisfactory. Twenty-one new trains are to form the equipment, and it would not be surprising if some of the passenger traffic were diverted from the Brighton to the S. E. section when the full service is in operation.[20]

*

On 10th July 1925 advertisements appeared in local newspapers advising the public of the commencement of electrified services to London on the 12th July 1925. The electric trains were scheduled to stop at all stations, but the public were assured that there would still be a considerable saving in time on the journey to London because of the increased acceleration of the electric trains. This would more than compensate for the delays caused by the stops, which were in any case limited to twenty seconds at each station. On the St Paul's to Crystal Palace High Level route, trains would run every 20 minutes throughout the day, from 6.03am to 12.23am. Trains would be scheduled to leave at 3, 23 and 43 minutes past the hour.[21] On Sundays, however, the trains were run at 30 minute intervals.

When the new services came into operation on the 12th July there was initially a series of breakdowns caused by blown fuses on the trains, sticking brakes and one case of a traction motor burning out. After several days, however, satisfactory running was achieved.[22] It was not until August 1925 that the first fatality occurred on the High Level line when a labourer, Thomas Henry Furner, was knocked down and killed by one of the new electric trains. The accident occurred at night near Upper Sydenham station at a point 100 yards from the entrance to the Paxton Tunnel. Thomas Furner and some other men were in a hut preparing their tools whilst waiting for the electric current to be cut off so that they could work in the tunnel. At about 12.15am Furner left the hut and was later found at the side of the line with head and face injuries. A witness stated that the 12.03 from St Paul's to the Crystal Palace passed the hut at 12.25am. The driver of this train, Ernest James Watson, said that he noticed nothing unusual on the journey. He was informed of the accident when his train reached the Crystal Palace but was unable to find any marks on the carriages. However, as the 12.3am from St Paul's was the only train to pass the hut at the time the labourer was knocked down, the Coroner assumed that this train must have been responsible for the accident. A

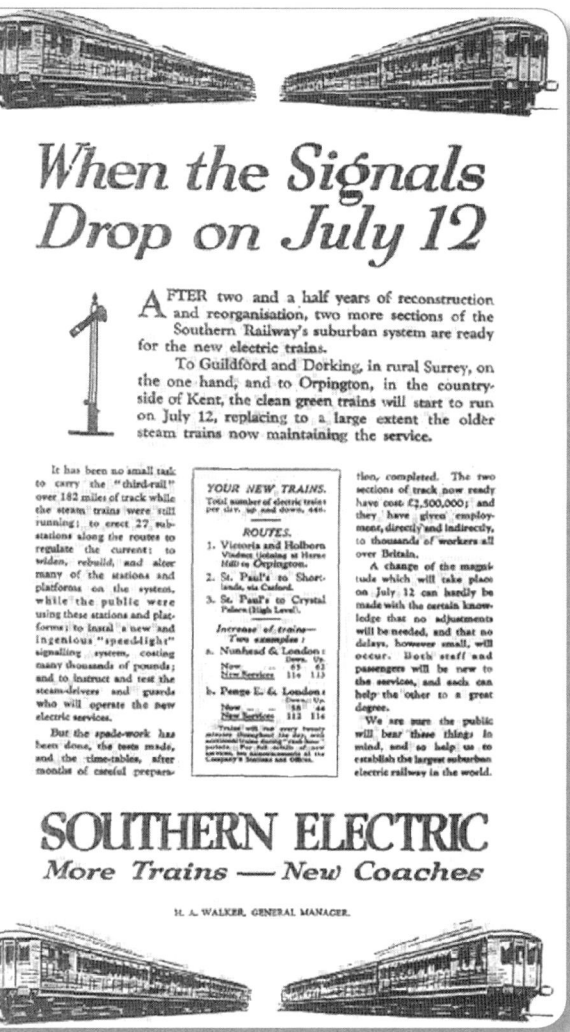

Plate 59 - Posters such as this publicised the introduction of electric train services on 12th July 1925 to Guildford, Dorking, Orpington and the Crystal Palace High Level stations.

verdict of accidental death was eventually given.[23]

If the Southern Railway had hoped to recuperate some of the money spent on electrifying the Crystal Palace High Level line it was to be disappointed, for electrification did not significantly increase either the revenue or the number of passengers using the line. In 1926 a traffic survey showed that there were only thirteen passengers per train on departures from Crystal Palace, and even fewer people arrived at the station. At Upper Sydenham station only 211 passengers departed and only 216 arrived on the day of the survey.[24] Perhaps passengers preferred the transport facilities offered by the local bus and tram services, which were now gaining a foothold in the area.

*

Electrification was not always a comfortable business for the traveller. The trains were flimsy wooden affairs, reconstructed from the stock used for steam operation, and they creaked and pitched and banged with the electric motors built into them. But it represented a great and unquestionable improvement on the older means of traction, in cleanliness, speed and punctuality.[25]

*

Plate 60 - London Transport tramcar No.145 on 18th October 1950 working route 58 near Lordship Lane station. Naturally, the trams took traffic from the local railways.

Pamlin Prints

The End of the Crystal Palace

Although passenger traffic on the High Level line did not increase noticeably following electrification, the frequent train service between St Paul's and the High Level station proved helpful in bringing visitors to the Crystal Palace. This fact was acknowledged by the press in 1926, when the Palace significantly reduced the deficit that had been incurred during 1925.[26] However, more income would have been generated if the Crystal Palace had been served by a direct tram service. An attempt to introduce such a service had been made in 1923, when it was suggested that trams should run from the West Norwood terminus to the Crystal Palace.[27] This scheme did not proceed, but the idea was reactivated in 1929 when the London County Council met to discuss the possible construction of new tramways to the Crystal Palace. However, both Camberwell Council and the Dulwich College Trustees raised objections to the proposals, and consequently a tram service to the Crystal Palace was not introduced.[28]

In December 1928 the funeral of 'Curly' Latter, a guard on the High Level line, took place at Elmers End Cemetery. William Latter was 54 years old at the time of his death and had worked on the railway for over thirty years. He first worked as a porter at Catford before becoming a guard at Victoria. After spending twenty-four years at Victoria he then joined the staff at the Crystal Palace High Level station. He was a popular member of staff and the funeral was attended by many members of the Southern Railway.[29]

The following year the station master at Crystal Palace High Level station retired after fifty years service as a railwayman. Mr W. J. Wood was presented with a gold medal by Sir Herbert Walker, the general manager of the Southern Railway, in recognition of his long service. Mr Wood first joined the railway in 1879 in Hastings, and from there he went to Winchester, Rye, Aldershot, Woolwich and Cannon Street. At the age of 25 he was appointed station master at Coombe Lane station on the Croydon and Oxted line, and then worked as station master at Grove Ferry, Crayford, and Bromley before moving to the High Level station where he acted as station master for ten years.

Mr Wood came from a railway family. His father completed fifty-one years service, his son was employed in the head office of the Southern Railway and both of his brothers were also railwaymen. Sadly his retirement only lasted until 1932 when his death was announced in the local press.[30]

Shortly after the retirement of Mr Woods, the station master, the Southern Railway was involved in three minor court cases, one in 1931, one in 1932 and the last in 1934, in connection with incidents on the High Level railway. The first concerned the transferability of tickets, when a man was charged with unlawfully transferring the return half of a workman's ticket to another person. Details of the case were given in the press:

✳

A solicitor, supporting the proceedings on behalf of the Southern Railway Company, said the defendant took a workman's ticket from Upper Sydenham to St Paul's. The return half was given up by a lady who was questioned by the collector. When he was afterwards interviewed, the defendant admitted that he gave away the ticket, but said that he had not read the regulations and was not aware that it was not transferable. The solicitor drew attention to the conditions which were printed on the rear of Southern Railway tickets:

NOT TRANSFERABLE
Issued subject to the Bye-Laws, Regulations, Notices and Conditions published in the Company's Time Tables, Bills and Notices

The defendant said that it was an oversight on his part, but a fine of 5 shillings was imposed and one guinea costs.[31]

✳

The second minor case occurred as a result of an incident in the yard of the Crystal Palace High Level station. The section of yard adjacent to Farquhar Road was poorly lit at night, there being only two lights on the High Level railway station wall, and one gas lamp provided by Lambeth Council which gave feeble illumination. At 11.55pm the local policeman was on duty in Farquhar Road when he heard voices in the yard of the railway station. Looking over the wall the policeman saw

Plate 61 - Taken from a postcard dating from the pre-grouping era, this view of the interior of the High Level station clearly shows the glass globes that were used for illumination. Some were allegedly stolen, as recounted on this page. Here SE&CR A1 Class 0-4-4T No.625 waits with a train for Victoria and creates a smoke haze for good measure. *Lens of Sutton Association*

two youths who were looking at some lock-up shops which adjoined the yard, however, when challenged the youths were able to disappear into the darkness. In order to apprehend the intruders the policeman obtained the assistance of another constable and a railway porter, and together they searched the yard. They eventually found the youths hiding in a recess in the wall underneath a lock-up shop. When the defendants appeared in court they gave evidence on their own behalf, stating that they only went into the yard for a lark. The magistrate told the defendants that, 'You acted in a stupid way. Don't do it again.' However, in view of the fact that no other offence had been committed, the magistrate ordered the defendants to be discharged.[32]

Old photographs of the High Level station show that parts of the station were illuminated by glass globes. On the 31st July 1934 police found a number of these globes stored in the garage of a house in Lansdowne Place, Upper Norwood. The globes were of varying sizes but were all marked with the initials 'SR', although an attempt had been made to burn off the initials from some of the smaller ones. The garage owner insisted that he had bought the globes from a rag and bone dealer, but he denied knowing that they had been stolen from the Crystal Palace station. He said that he had paid sixpence each for the small globes and one shilling and sixpence for the large one. When the garage proprietor subsequently appeared at Penge Magistrates Court he was identified by a Southern Railway foreman who confirmed that the man frequently visited the High Level station, and that he had previously worked for the railway company. When it was revealed that he had a previous conviction for aiding and abetting another person to commit fraud by travelling on the railway without paying the appropriate fare, the magistrate imposed a fine of £3 or 25 days imprisonment.[33]

Of all the evening events held at the Crystal Palace few were more popular than the firework displays which were held every Thursday at dusk during the firework season. These displays had been held continuously since 1865, except for a short interval before and after the war and during the period of hostilities.

*

Each year during this long period a new subject has been found for the spectacular main set-piece. Portraits of notabilities, topical events, puzzle pictures, a wreck, a lifeboat rescue, volcanic eruptions, as well as many others have been used, but there is, perhaps, no type of subject offering such scope to the pyrotechnic artist as does a battle. The Armada, the Nile, the First of June, Trafalgar (during its centenary year), Jutland, Zeebrugge and the Dardanelles all made successful pictures, as did the Zeppelin raid on London.[34]

*

The firework displays generated pleasure traffic for the Southern Railway, for huge crowds were always in attendance. This resulted in cheap day return tickets being available between Crystal Palace High and Low Level stations and London, although the fares were increased by one penny from both stations in 1932 in order to make the inward cheap day return fare to London the same as the outward return fare.[35] It was the policy of the Southern Railway to encourage pleasure traffic, and consequently advertisements regularly appeared in the press giving details of cheap return tickets from all of its stations to the major south coast resorts. From the High Level station it was possible to travel to Whitstable and Herne Bay for a return fare of five shillings, or Margate, Broadstairs and Ramsgate for five shillings and sixpence. For the same fare Bognor Regis could be reached by travelling from Crystal Palace Low Level station.[36]

In January 1936 a meeting of Penge Urban District Council was held to discuss the finances of the Crystal Palace and to elect a trustee. During the course of the meeting it was noted that the grounds of the Crystal Palace were not fully open to the public, and that the people of Penge '... felt it to be a crying shame for the excellent gardens to be closed in the form they were'. It was also noted that a financial loss had been incurred in the previous year, and that this had resulted in a decrease in the rateable value of the Crystal Palace.[37]

Nevertheless events continued to be held within the Crystal Palace building. In November 1936 the Southern Railway was required to run six special trains in order to bring 5,000 exhibits of poultry, pigeons and rabbits to the Palace for an international show which was held annually.[38] This was to be followed by a cat show which was to be held on the 2nd December 1936, but this event was destined never to take place.

On the night of Monday, 30th November 1936 the Crystal Palace was destroyed by fire. A discarded cigarette, an electrical fault, an insurance swindle, or sabotage, the true reason for the fire has never been established. It was, however, a spectacular inferno, the likes of which had never been seen before. The flames quickly devoured the glass and metal structure, but the glow of the fire could be seen 50 miles away in Brighton, and it was reported that 80 miles away in mid-channel the pilot of an Imperial Airways plane flying at 7,000 feet could see the blaze.[39] Thousands of glass fragments were subsequently found in the surrounding roads, and a piece of metal was found as far away as Beckenham, although it had to be allowed to cool before it could be picked up. So many people attempted to make their way to Crystal Palace Parade that the roads became blocked and fire engines were held up. On one major road cars stretched back as far as Mitcham. Fortunately no lives were lost in the conflagration, but the fire left behind a blackened ruin with only the two huge water towers left standing.

When the fire took hold there were sets of old London, Chatham & Dover 6-wheel stock berthed in the sidings of the High Level station. These were kept in reserve for summer excursions, hop pickers' specials and national emergencies.[40] The stationmaster of the High Level station, Mr C. G. Allaston, gave the following account of the fire, and told of the use that the public made of these carriages:

*

The High Level station entrance is situated on the Parade and faces the Palace. With the congestion it was most difficult for passengers to leave the station, and another exit was used in Farquhar Road. This soon became as bad as the main exit, consequently another, the footbridge, was used, well down behind the huge mass of people then gathered. This continued until the last train at 12.36am.

Some 2,000 to 3,000 people stormed the Goods Yard, climbing up on trucks and steam trains standing out in the sidings, so many venturing near the live rails that it became necessary to send for our police to control the crowds. Nothing could be done to get such a large number out, so they were permitted to remain, the position, by the way, giving an excellent view.

The London Fire Brigade made their headquarters in the south side booking office and waiting rooms, taking full possession of the National telephone until late in the afternoon of the next day. Just after 2am on Tuesday we were honoured with a visit by the Duke of Kent, who was very interested in the Brigade's methods and the arrangements in hand.

After the last train (11.27pm) had left, about 70 passengers presented themselves for all stations to London, and a special was run at midnight to get them home. All had been so hemmed in with the crowd that some said they had been struggling for over an hour to get to the station. In all there were 91 fire engines, 381 officers, and firemen from all parts …[41]

*

Thousands of passengers were dealt with at both the High Level and Low Level stations. During the week following over 5,000 sightseers were booked away from these two stations.[42] But this was the end of an era for the Southern Railway. Bank holidays would no longer attract huge crowds to the Crystal Palace and there would be no more exhibitions. Thus it was no surprise that from 1936 there was a severe reduction in the number of passengers using the Low and High Level stations.

Plate 62 - This slightly fuzzy pre-November 1936 view shows the position of both the High Level station and the Crystal Palace, separated by The Parade. There was a subway under The Parade to give passengers direct access from the station to the Crystal Palace.   *Crystal Palace Museum*

Plate 63 - The station and signal box facing Nunhead. This affords a good view of the size of the station building.

Lordship Lane in Southern Railway days, c.1928-30

Plate 64 - Lordship Lane station and the rear of the signal box from an adjacent footpath.   *Pictures from Roger Carpenter*

The War Years

The destruction of the Crystal Palace, and the consequent loss of potential railway passengers, was to have an adverse effect on the profitability of the Southern Railway High Level line. As a result of the failure of previous companies to extend the line beyond Crystal Palace, the Southern was forced to rely heavily upon local commuters to provide income for the line. The grounds of the Crystal Palace were, of course, still open to the public, and when in April 1937 the first motor racing event took place on the new Crystal Palace road racing circuit, between 40,000 and 50,000 people attended this race meeting. There were, however, alternative means of transport now available to compete with railway travel, and at the time that the motor racing event took place the motor car had become the preferred means of transportation.

*

Traffic conditions reminiscent of the occasion when the Crystal Palace was burned down were again seen in Norwood on Saturday when the first motor racing event took place on the new Crystal Palace road-racing circuit …. There were thousands of motor cars in all roads leading to the Crystal Palace. Anerley Hill was absolutely blocked by traffic for a considerable time, and cars stretched from the Palace along Westow Hill and Central Hill almost down to Beulah Hill. About 1200 cars were parked at the Penge entrance, and in Thicket Road, Anerley, vehicles were parked three deep, leaving only room for a single line of traffic. Motor cyclists rode on the pavements.[43]

*

There was one event in 1937, however, which proved to be extremely beneficial to the Southern Railway. The Coronation of George VI took place in London on the 12th May, and to accommodate visitors the Southern ran a 24-hour train service commencing at 3am and continuing until 3am on the following day. Two hundred and twenty-five special early morning trains were run into London from all stations, extending as far as Exeter, in order to allow passengers who wished to see the procession the opportunity to arrive in London before 6am. Cheap day return tickets to London could also be purchased for all trains throughout the day. Visitors wishing to see the decorations and illuminations could purchase cheap day and half day tickets from all Southern Railway stations during the period Thursday, 13th May to Saturday, 22nd May.[44]

But the High Level line attracted fewer and fewer passengers, and complaints were again raised in the local press about the high fares charged from the High Level station:

*

The biggest objection to the old Crystal Palace being used for a world youth centre is rail transport and rightly …. The fares charged in this district are higher than in other districts …. The rail route from the High Level station is

Plate 65 - Upper Sydenham in September 1934, some nine years after the line was electrified. The extensions to the old platform are clearly visible and the original platform lamps have been swept away in favour of the Southern's own style. Signals and signal box are gone, too; the Up starter and Lordship Lane distant just visible at the tunnel mouth in *Plate 52* have been removed, as has the quite prominent Down starter in *Plate 42*.   *Lens of Sutton Association*

very indirect, the distance to town is 9¾ miles, and we pay 11d; for the straight Richmond run, 9¾ miles, it costs only 9½d, and actually for the same amount one can travel 13½ miles to Hounslow from Waterloo .... It is time something was done.[45]

*

In December 1938 the press reported that there had been an epidemic of railway station robberies in the area, and that the Crystal Palace High Level station was the latest place to be burgled. The thieves had apparently locked themselves in the waiting room and then forced open the door leading to the booking office. When the burglary was discovered by the head porter, it was found that although the takings in the safe had not been touched, small sums were missing, including money collected for the staff football pontoon.[46]

Shortly after this burglary, in February 1939, Mr E. C. Scott, a guard at the High Level station, received a posthumous award from the General Manager of the Southern Railway. It was said of Guard Scott, who had died a month earlier, that he had taken great interest in noting passenger conditions at stations and in drawing attention to cases where the provision of new direction signs would have been of assistance to passengers. During 1938 no less than nine of Guard Scott's suggestions were adopted, and although each of these was not of great importance in itself, in aggregate Guard Scott's suggestions proved of real value to the Company. The General Manager subsequently sent a cheque for

£5, the amount of the award, to Guard Scott's widow.[47]

World War II caused severe delays to all trains running on the Southern, and eventually the train services on the High Level line were reduced when, in January 1940, an hourly service was introduced at off peak times and on Sundays. In March 1940 the Southern Railway Company issued a press statement about the overall situation:

*

THE "SOUTHERN" AND ITS PASSENGERS

Since the outbreak of War, and the imposition of the "black-out" we have seen with great regret our much prized punctuality records going by the board, particularly during the evenings. These records were second to none in peace-time.

The winter is passing, summertime is here and the "black-out" problem will become less acute. But the stream of special trains for troops, sailors, airmen, ammunition supplies and Government stores continues unabated, and these trains must have precedence. So will you understand if your train is a bit late sometimes? We are as alive to the value of punctuality to business people as ever, and there is no detail of our train performance that we do not watch every day and every hour.

We have profited by experience and have done much to beat the effect of the "black-out". More and more trains

Plate 66 - Staff posed for a photograph at Crystal Palace High Level on 21st May 1944 with 'Brighton Belle' set in background.   *Gary Cross*

are being equipped with white lights, and the lighting of stations and goods yards is gradually being improved. But there must still be delay and interference with regular running at times when the pressure of Government traffic is most acute, and odd minutes here and there become a formidable pile when added together. These minutes cannot easily be recovered.

Most of our passengers know our record well enough to trust us not to condemn them to any delays and irritations which can be avoided. It is still "Southern FOR Service" even though it is "Southern ON Service".

From THE MANAGEMENT ON BEHALF OF ALL THE SOUTHERN RAILWAY STAFF [48]

＊

Shortly after the introduction of 'black-out regulations on the railways, an extraordinary event occurred late at night in a Southern Railway carriage on the High Level line. The train was travelling towards Lordship Lane station when a man opened the door of a compartment and climbed along the off-side footboard of the train. He then proceeded to make faces at a young couple through the window of their compartment. This behaviour was apparently due to a dispute over who should accompany the girl home after all three had attended a local dance. On re-entering the train the man threw the girl onto the seat of the compartment and then attempted to throw her companion out of the carriage window, which was broken during the struggle. By this time the guard had been alerted, but as he tried to take the name and address of the assailant, the man suddenly opened the offside door of the compartment, jumped out on the line, and then disappeared into the darkness. He was, however, subsequently arrested and appeared at Lambeth Police Court where he was fined a total of £6 or one month's imprisonment for disorderliness.[49]

In 1941 further cuts were made to the High Level line services when on the 6th January the branch was reduced to a shuttle service between the High Level station and Nunhead. From Nunhead connections were made with the Catford Loop service, every 20 minutes at peak periods, and hourly at other times.[50] This situation lasted until 1944, when in April of that year the Southern Railway announced that '... the passenger services on the Nunhead to Crystal Palace (High Level) section … will be withdrawn on Monday, May 22nd. The stations affected will be Crystal Palace (High Level), Upper Sydenham, Lordship Lane and Honor Oak. Comparatively small use is now made of this line by the public, and good alternative routes are available by rail and road. The closing of this branch line is solely due to the manpower position.' [51]

The High Level station was once again closed during wartime and the staff were transferred to other stations. But before leaving, a presentation was made to the stationmaster, Mr William Tytherleigh, who had been promoted to stationmaster at Streatham Common. Mr Tytherleigh entered the railway service in 1899 at Ockley in Surrey. He then worked at Streatham, Sydenham and Peckham Rye stations before becoming stationmaster at Fleet in Hampshire. He then spent seven years as stationmaster at the High Level station. Mr

Tytherleigh was presented with a briefcase by Mr P. Nunn, District Superintendent and also received an umbrella from the staff. Several employees spoke favourably about Mr Tytherleigh at the meeting, and compliments were also received from the firm of W. H. Smith & Son, and from the local coal merchants. Mr Tytherleigh's last words to the staff were 'I wish you goodbye, good luck, clear signals, and a good run'. [52]

With the line closed further use was made of the sidings at the High Level station. Previously carriages had been stored there for use on excursions and for hop picker specials. Now, however, buffet cars, pullman cars and a 5-BEL Pullman unit No.3052 were shunted into the sidings.[53] Pullman carriages *Audrey* (No.280) and *Vera* (No284), which had been damaged in an air raid near Victoria in 1940, were eventually returned to service seven years later.[54] The interior of the High Level station was also used to store carriages:

＊

Silence hung over the station, once filled with the shunting of trains and the clatter and chatter of passengers. Instead of the "P" trains pulling out of Platforms 1 and 2 for Nunhead, they remained stationary on the rails.[55]

＊

In October 1944 the *Norwood News* published an article on the air raid shelter which had been set up by Camberwell Council in the ornamental subway under Crystal Palace Parade connecting the High Level station to the Crystal Palace. The red and cream brickwork arches had been filled in to form bays, enabling up to one hundred people from the Norwood district to seek protection against enemy action. It was reported that on the first day of the flying bomb attacks a 'Shelter' notice appeared above the northern entrance to the High Level station, and that as many as two hundred people attempted to use the shelter at the height of the bombing. Families arriving at the shelter were pleased to find a well stocked canteen run by Mrs M. Sampson, who kept it open from five o'clock until nine in the morning, and from five until eleven at night.[56]

This article prompted Mr Tytherleigh, the former stationmaster at the High Level station, to send a letter to the *Norwood News*:

＊

In your issue of October 27th you published an article on the shelter at Crystal Palace High Level station, in which it is stated that on the first day of the flying bomb attacks the notice 'Shelter' appeared above the northern entrance to the High Level station. May I point out that the shelter was already in use several years ago, and that the notice has been over the northern entrance during that time, and has been illuminated at night during the time that all alerts were operating?

When the shelter was completed bunks were installed, and as the Borough of Camberwell A.R.P Service in the district was very short of personnel, a request was made to the Southern Railway for the lights to be switched on each night and extinguished at dawn by the staff of the High Level station. The shelter at this time was open continuously. Later, owing to the damage to fittings etc. at the various public shelters, it was decided that many

Plate 67 - Ex-LSWR three-coach electric set No.4196 in Crystal Palace High Level station. Note air raid damage to glass panels in the roof, and the wooden planked platform.   *Gary Cross*

of these should be closed, except during the period that warnings were in force, and the shelter at the High Level was one which was closed.

The Southern Railway undertook that their staff should open the shelter and switch on the lights upon the sounding of warnings, and close down and switch off the lights when the 'Raiders passed' was sounded, and this was done without fail at all times within the 24 hours, right down to the time the High Level station was closed for passenger traffic. After this took place I do not know what arrangements were made.

As your paragraph may lead to a belief that the undertaking given by the railway company was not carried out, and in fairness to the staff concerned, who so faithfully carried out the duty, sometimes at some risk to themselves, I suggest that you should, with your usual courtesy, make it clear that the shelter was available in every case of need, right from the time of its completion.

W. TYTHERLEIGH - late station master High Level Station[57]

*

Three months before the end of World War II an obituary appeared in the local press for Mr W. Richards, who had been a popular passenger guard at the High Level station. Mr Richards obtained employment on the railway as a boy and worked as a porter and shunter. Eventually he became a guard when the electric trains came to the High Level line, and he was well

known to those who travelled regularly between Norwood and Victoria. Mr Richards was a member of the National Union of Railwaymen and had qualified for the fifty years long service gold medal. However, he never received the award due to circumstances brought about by the war. He was considered one of the 'old team' at the High Level station, and had only retired from the Southern Railway the previous year when the station was closed down.[58]

The financial viability of the High Level line had always depended upon the success of the Crystal Palace, and when the war ended the prospects for the re-development of the Crystal Palace grounds seemed quite promising. The Trustees were keen to develop the site; indeed, ambitious plans had already been put forward by Sir Henry Buckland, the General Manager, for the development of the grounds to include exhibition halls, a skating rink, a swimming pool and a vast arena for all sporting events. He considered that financing the work would not prove difficult as '... this is one of the finest business propositions ever contemplated, and no man of discernment will hesitate to further such an attractive scheme.' [59]

Neighbouring local authorities were generally supportive of the development proposals, but they were also prepared to enforce the 1914 Act against the Trustees in the event of non-compliance. The Act specified that the public should be given full access to the grounds, and that the grounds should be maintained and managed as a place for education and recreation and for the promotion of industry, commerce and art. However, non-compliance seemed unlikely in view of the fact that the Trustees were supportive of Sir Henry Buckland's proposals. The Southern Railway Company was, of course, likely to benefit from any increase in traffic generated by re-development of the Crystal Palace grounds in the event of the High Level line being re-opened.

The End of the Southern

In late 1945 Mrs J. Adamson MP sent a letter to the Ministry of War Transport concerning the continuing closure of the Crystal Palace to Nunhead High Level line. Concerned, in particular, about the closure of Honor Oak and Lordship Lane stations Mrs Adamson wrote:

＊

I also understand that in view of the late sittings of the House it would be a considerable service to certain members if late trains could call at Honor Oak and Lordship Lane stations which are now closed. Is there any prospect of their re-opening? [60]

＊

The Ministry of War Transport forwarded the letter to the Secretary of the Railway Executive Committee for observations, who in turn sent it to the General Manager's office of the Southern Railway. In due course, the Railway Executive Committee received the following reply:

＊

Referring to your letter of the 18th December, it was hoped that it would be possible to restore the passenger

train service on the Nunhead to Crystal Palace (HL) Line on January 7th next, but the engineering work involved, particularly in connection with war damage at Lordship Lane station, is such that it has been found necessary to postpone the re-opening date. It is hoped that this will be about February 15th, but I will advise you definitely as soon as I am in a position to do so, and then give fuller information of the services we are able to run. [61]

＊

A further communication was sent from the General Manager's office to the Railway Executive Committee on the 6th February 1946:

＊

Further to my letter of the 22nd December arrangements are being made to re-instate the passenger train service on the Nunhead to Crystal Palace (HL) line on and from Monday 4th March all trains calling at all stations on the branch. The service will comprise 3 trains per hour during the business periods and two per hour at other times and on Sundays. The last train for Crystal Palace (HL) on weekdays will leave Nunhead at 11.51pm and form a connection with the 11.25pm from Holborn Viaduct. [62]

＊

When this information was conveyed to Mrs Adamson by the Ministry of War Transport she made a further request:

＊

I am in receipt of yours of the 27th February about the Nunhead / Crystal Palace line re-opening, for which I thank you. As, however, the last train leaves Holborn

Plate 68 - Crystal Palace High Level looking towards Paxton tunnel on 3rd October 1953.   *R C Riley; The Transport Treasury*

Plate 69 - The stationmaster's house and wooden booking office at Honor Oak two days before closure. Tickets were eventually sold on the platform. The car numberplate reads TL 4706, the van WMP 382.

Lens of Sutton Association
❖

Viaduct at 11.25 it does not help with my problem of reaching home at *Forest Hill* via Lordship Lane station ... I hope and trust that extra facilities for a later service will soon be available for those of us who live on this particular line.[63]

∗

When the General Manager's office of the Southern Railway was asked to respond to this request, the following reply was sent to the Railway Executive Committee:

∗

So far as the Nunhead / Crystal Palace (HL) route is concerned, which serves Lordship Lane, the late trains are very poorly patronised, and the respective loadings of the four last services from Nunhead (connecting with trains from Holborn Viaduct) on April 1st were 3, 2, 1 and 2 passengers only. In the circumstances the running of late trains on the route cannot be recommended, particularly in view of the coal position.[64]

∗

The closure of the High Level line during World War II caused severe problems for rush hour travellers to the City. Before the war there had been six trains an hour from the Low Level station, and three from the High Level, but the closure reduced this service to four trains an hour from the Low Level station. There were complaints that these trains were irregularly spaced, causing a delay to travellers to intermediate stations. It was therefore not surprising that there were calls for the pre-war service at the Low Level station to be resumed, and for the High Level line to be re-opened.[65]

When the line was eventually re-opened on 4th March 1946 the Crystal Palace High Level station was in a most dilapidated state. Although there had been no direct hits on the station during air raids, vibration caused by anti-aircraft guns had broken many of the glass panes in the roof and no attempt had been made to carry out repairs. The north end of the station was in such poor condition that it had been abandoned, leaving birds to nest in the ceilings undisturbed. A description of the

station at this time is given in *London's Local Railways*:

∗

Rain poured down through the shattered roof at High Level encouraging a luxuriant growth of ferns and fungi on rotting timber platforms beneath which rats, far outnumbering the passengers, scurried and scavenged unhindered ... safety nets drooped from the roof to protect passengers from falling debris. At night it was one of the most eerie public places in London.[66]

∗

This dilapidated building was a magnet for small boys, and it was not long before the local policeman, PC Edds, apprehended a 12-year-old who he found sitting on the safety railings over the roof of the station. The boy had a kit bag beside him which was subsequently found to be full of lead. As he admitted that the lead had come from the roof, he was subsequently charged with the theft of a quantity of the material valued at 18s 3d.[67]

After the High Level train service was restored in 1946 the trains were poorly patronised, and it was found sufficient to run only four-coach trains at any time of day. Traffic had been lost during the wartime closure as passengers had found other routes. In addition, part of the area served by the line had been severely damaged in air raids and all of the stations on the line were in need of urgent repair work.[68] Despite the difficulties faced by the railway company in running services from both the High and Low Level stations, complaints to local newspapers continued to be published.

∗

I have noticed that general improvements have taken place of the London Passenger Transport Board's vehicles in the past few weeks, including more trains, buses and coaches, etc. The Southern Railway, however, seems very slow in restoring their pre-war local services, particularly to the Crystal Palace. The service to Victoria from the Low Level is still at only fifty per cent of the former number, due to the curtailing of the Beckenham Junction trains at Crystal Palace instead of running through to Victoria. The High

Level line has been re-opened, but the service provided is very poor, and although the official excuse is that no more trains can be passed through Blackfriars, due to signalling reasons, this certainly cannot apply during the non-rush hours, when most services are cut by half. Trusting that your newspaper will draw attention to this fact, so that passengers may have better services in this district as well as others.[69]

*

Although passenger services were limited, there was a daily freight service from Herne Hill coal yard. This was hauled by an ex-SE&CR Class C 0-6-0 locomotive which always utilised the turntable at the southern end of the Crystal Palace High Level station to save running back tender first to Herne Hill.[70]

In May 1947 services were severely disrupted at Upper Sydenham station when slippage occurred from a tip formed from rubble from bombing raids. The press gave the height of the tip as being 150ft above the station and the slippage caused movement of the up platform and ladies waiting room. It was found necessary to demolish the waiting room as it was being pushed steadily forward and the platform had to be barricaded with 100 tons of iron in the form of old railway lines to prevent further movement.

In order to give warning of further slippage, watchmen kept an all night vigil at the station and men were employed to shore up the railway bridge and the nearby signal boxes. Movement of the rubble was first noticed in March 1946, but it was not until a platelayer on his way to work found the

station railings and platform bulging dangerously that action was taken. Mr Holdsworth, a porter at the station, said that for him the first indication of danger was when the gas failed, as the landslide had broken the gas pipe. He told reporters that in his opinion the slippage would have been far worse but for the fact that a number of strong trees growing on the bank had stopped its progress. Services on the line were delayed for two days and passengers had to be taken to their destinations by special buses. It was also necessary to switch off the current temporarily to enable men to work safely. Nearby householders were concerned to note pieces of rubble falling from the top of the tip. They were also plagued with rats and crickets which were no doubt disturbed by the slippage.[71]

The year 1947 was also noted for atrocious weather conditions. Heavy snow and rain, which fell in the Penge and Anerley area in March, caused conditions which long-service transport employees described as the worst ever experienced. Milk deliveries were affected in the area as milk trains were unable to get through, and at the Low Level station the station master noted that ice on the live rail was a quarter of an inch thick. Passengers waited at the top of the stairs, not knowing when, and on which platform, the next train would arrive. At the High Level station a foreman took the place of a guard who had been held up. He acted as guard on the 5.46am train to the City but it took him six hours to travel to London and back. On the return journey the icy conditions caused the train to breakdown at Nunhead, so another train was coupled to it. However, the load was far too high and a complaint from the

Plate 70 - The Down platform waiting rooms at Upper Sydenham in the early 1950s.   *Lens of Sutton Association*

local power station was received. It was therefore necessary for a light engine to pilot the train to the Crystal Palace, where it arrived four and a quarter hours late.[72]

In October of the same year staff at the Crystal Palace High Level station gathered to make a presentation to Mr Ernest W. Pettitt, who had worked on the railways for forty two years, thirty five of them as a carriage cleaner at the High Level station. Mr Pettitt first came to work at High Level in 1905 and stayed until he enlisted for the 1914-18 war. He returned in 1920 after being held as a prisoner of war for eighteen months. He was then promoted to leading cleaner, a job he held for eighteen years. Mr Pettitt informed his colleagues that in his time he had seen great changes at the station.

*

Gone were the days when the station master wore an imposing top hat and frock coat, when the plodding, noisy steam engines were filled with fashionable crowds, horse drawn cabs stood in a long rank outside the station, and when the London terminus was Elephant and Castle reached in half an hour .... 'Now I'm sorry I'm retiring,' he told a reporter, 'I'm still fit to carry on a job, but no doubt I'll find something else.' [73]

*

The development of the Crystal Palace site after the war would undoubtedly have brought visitors back to the Sydenham area, and would have increased the number of passengers using both the High and Low Level stations. Therefore, when the Government announced its intention to hold an International Exhibition in London, nearby local authorities, led by Camberwell Council, were keen to ensure that it was held on the Palace site. The Exhibition was scheduled to take place in 1951, so in early 1947 Camberwell Council made representations to the Prime Minister, the Lord President of the Council, the President of the Board of Trade and the Minister for Town and Country Planning that the Crystal Palace site should be used for the event. The Council also asked all of the metropolitan borough councils, the City of London Corporation, the London County Council, the Councils of the Boroughs of Beckenham, Croydon, Lambeth and Penge to support the bid.

There were several good reasons to hold the Festival of Britain, as the Exhibition was eventually to be called, at Crystal Palace. The Council pointed out that as the site belonged to the nation its acquisition would not involve any cost. It was already equipped with essential services, was ready for development, and would involve no displacement of people or industry. In addition, buildings erected for the purpose of the exhibition could be used for future events and for the recreation and education of the people. A site in Central London had none of these advantages and, moreover, any event in Central London would lead to an increase in the already bad traffic congestion.[74]

Although the arguments put forward for use of the Crystal Palace site were compelling, the Government eventually decided that they were not able to implement the Festival of Britain on the large scale that had been originally planned. It was therefore decided that the Festival should be on a much smaller scale, and as a consequence a site on the south bank of the Thames was eventually utilised.[75]

The lost opportunity to re-develop the Crystal Palace site sealed the fate of the High Level branch. Instead of the stations and electrical equipment being modernised in order to accommodate the thousands of passengers who would have flocked to the Crystal Palace, the railway continued to be poorly patronised and its assets continued to deteriorate. There was also a new post-war attitude to branch line railways which was summed up in a speech given to the Institute of Transport by Sir Cyril Hurcomb, Chairman of the British Transport Commission:

*

... Public transport can only pay its way if it is adequately patronised wherever it can give good service. Traders would be given freedom to choose the service most suited to their needs, but there would be nationwide integration of road, rail and waterway facilities. It is essential, however, that each step taken towards integration should add some thing to net revenue, either by increasing traffic, or by improving efficiency. The vast capital sunk in Britain's railway network can be made to yield a return only if it is used to somewhere near capacity.

The Road Transport Executive are being given traffic data in regard to railway branch lines which are unremunerative, so they can consider what it would cost them to convey the same traffic. At the same time the Railway Executive will calculate in each case what they would save by withdrawing a local service. On the other hand, there would be cases in which traffic now carried by road could be more advantageously handled by rail.

As the Commission extend their interests, interavailability between road and rail will develop. More bus services will centre on railway stations and scheduled connections between road and rail services will multiply. It will be necessary to accelerate the abandonment of unremunerative branch railway lines which in effect the public have themselves abandoned, and to close to passenger traffic many little-used intermediate stations, always provided adequate and equally convenient services can be given more economically by road.[76]

*

The British Transport Commission was a new organisation which had come into being as a result of the general election which was held when the war ended. A newly elected Labour Government, committed to the nationalisation of the railways, compulsorily purchased the railway companies by means of the Transport Act of 1947. The Government then abolished the old railway companies and the London Passenger Transport Board, and on 1st January 1948 brought into existence British Railways, a state railway system under the control of the British Transport Commission.[77]

The British Transport Commission was committed to the closure of unremunerative railway lines and also to the closure of under utilised stations. Between 1948 and 1959 it closed 2,944 miles of railway, either to passengers or to all traffic.[78] This strategy proved to be directly responsible for the discontinuation of the Crystal Palace High Level railway.

Plate 71 - The main entrance to Crystal Palace High Level station in Farquhar Road. Undated but probably after closure since the main doors appear closed and windows boarded up. The large billboard is advertising Guinness.

Lens of Sutton Association

❀ Pictorial survey ❀
Crystal Palace High Level

Plate 72 - Track recovery in progress at the High Level station. This is the only view available of the outside of the western wall of the train shed. Alongside this wall ran the headshunt for the coal yard and storage sidings; there was also a loading dock to serve the goods yard. The coal yard, which included small huts for the coal merchants, was mainly behind the photographer. *Lens of Sutton Association*

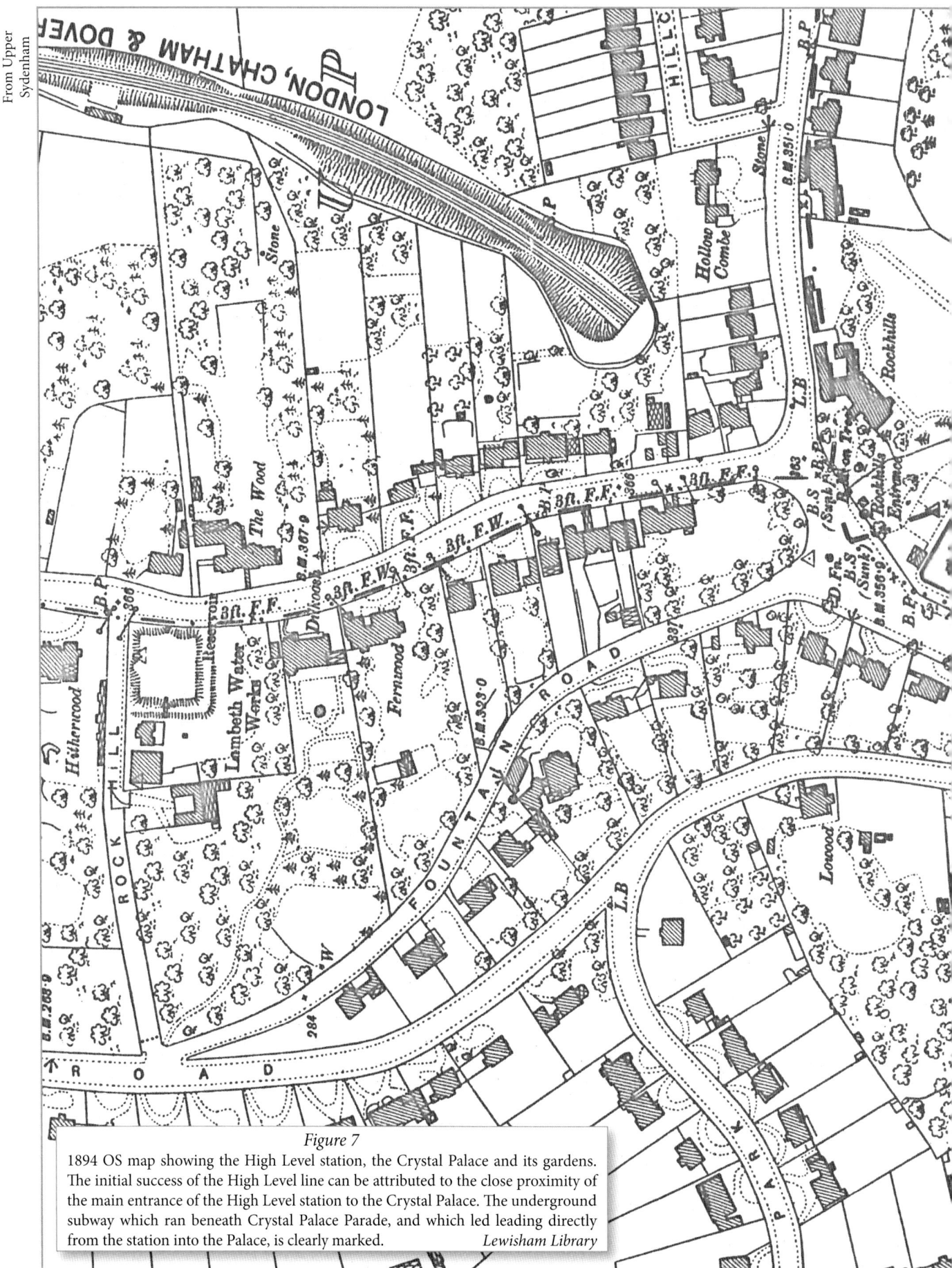

Figure 7

1894 OS map showing the High Level station, the Crystal Palace and its gardens. The initial success of the High Level line can be attributed to the close proximity of the main entrance of the High Level station to the Crystal Palace. The underground subway which ran beneath Crystal Palace Parade, and which led leading directly from the station into the Palace, is clearly marked.   *Lewisham Library*

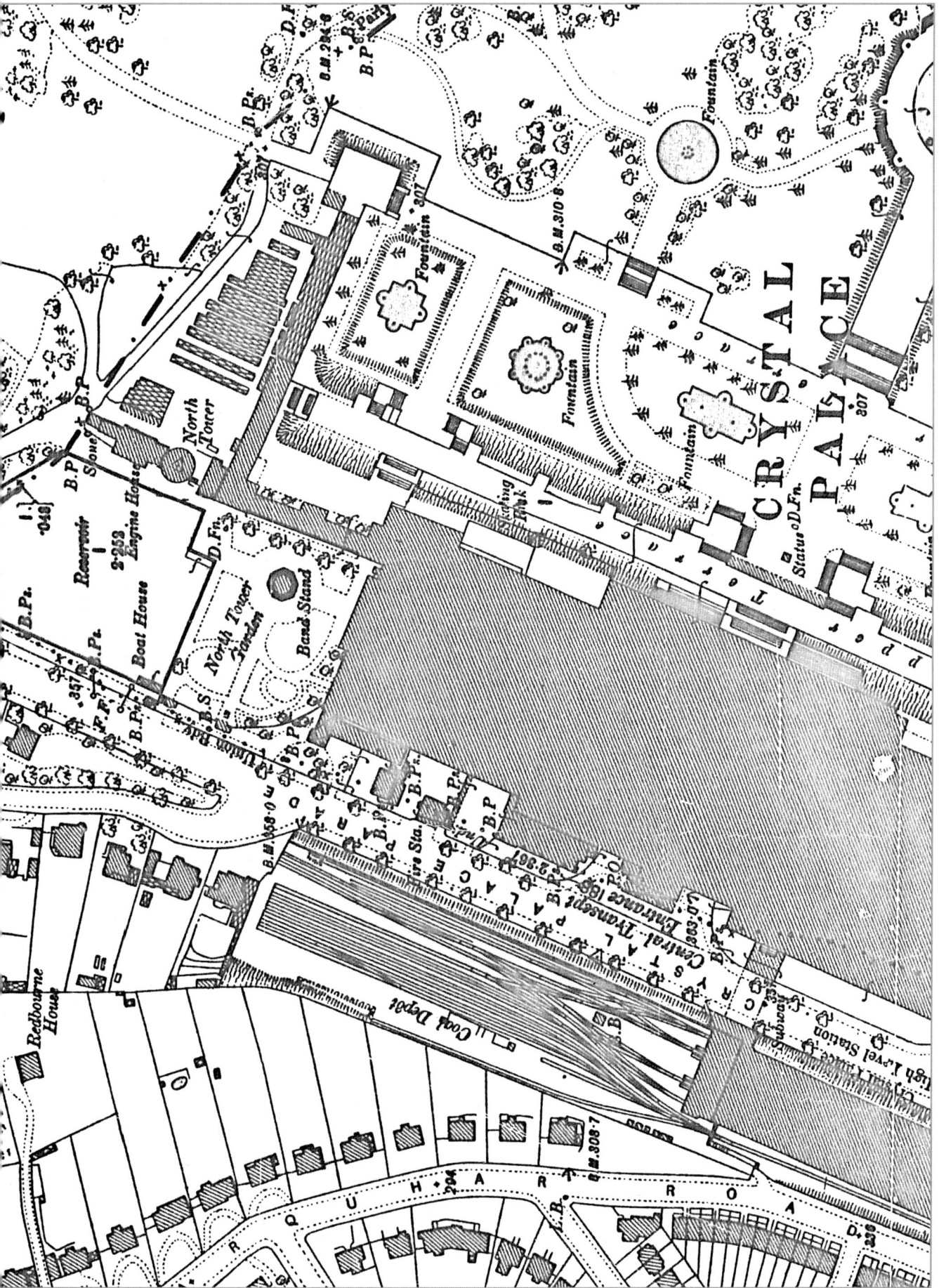

Plate 73 - The four platform roads came together at the southern end of the station and led onto a 45ft turntable. Note the ground discs protecting each platform line. The bridge carries Farquhar Road over the railway lines. The notice advises engine crews that their engines 'Must not blow off steam under this bridge'.

Lens of Sutton Association

Figure 8 - This plan of the High Level station is from *Railway & Travel Monthly* magazine of 1911.

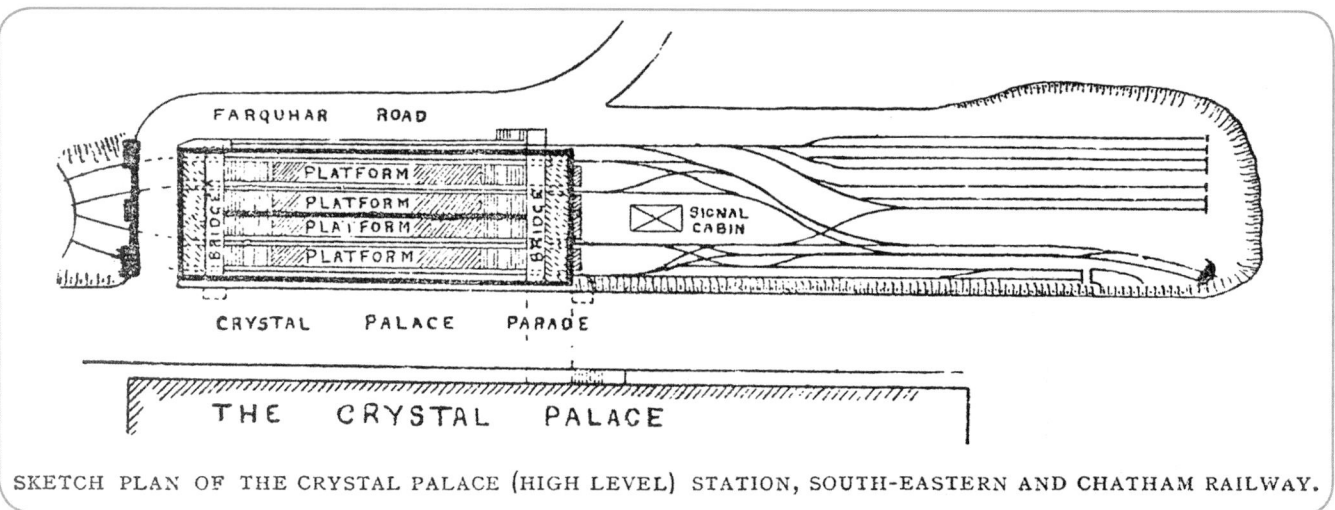

SKETCH PLAN OF THE CRYSTAL PALACE (HIGH LEVEL) STATION, SOUTH-EASTERN AND CHATHAM RAILWAY.

Plate 74 - Obviously installed for engine release purposes when the station was built, the turntable was usable throughout the years of electrification. Here No.31576, one of two Class C locomotives that hauled the Palace Centenarian on 19th September 1954, is using it.

R C Riley; The Transport Treasury

Plate 75 - The southern concourse showing stairs down to the platforms and plenty of billboards. The doors at the far end of the concourse led to a side entrance which opened onto Crystal Palace Parade. *Lens of Sutton Association*

Plate 76 - The north end of the High Level station. The view is undated but does show the rear of signals at the ends of the platform lines. Each line appears to be equipped with a short-arm semaphore, presumably for normal passenger train departures, and an O-shaped shunting disc. *SECR Society collection*

Plate 77 - A solitary mineral wagon stands in the coal yard. There is a road vehicle behind and to the left of the crane but no other signs of life. The interlaced turnout in the foreground is probably the most interesting feature of this photograph. There are other examples along the branch.   *Lens of Sutton Association*

Plate 78 - Busier times on Platform 1 at Crystal Palace, albeit on the last day of service. The young enthusiast in the bottom right corner is no doubt being introduced to the delights of 4-SUB electric unit No.4107. Sadly, he will see no more at this station after this day, 18th September 1954.

Mile Post 92½ Picture Library; A W V Mace

Plate 79 - The signalbox and approach to the High Level station on the last day of service. Locomotive-hauled carriage set No.468 stands in the storage sidings.

Mile Post 92½ Picture Library; A W V Mace

❧ *Chapter Six* ❧

FINAL CLOSURE

In July 1949 it was announced that a Working Party of Railway and London Transport Executives had proposed a £340 million programme of improvement and additions to London's transport system, to be undertaken over a period of between 20 and 30 years. Amongst the 'first priority' projects put forward was a tube railway from London to East Croydon, with mention also being made of a possible tube to the Crystal Palace. Referring to this possibility the Working Party report noted that:

*

Representations have been made for some time past by local authorities and other responsible bodies for improved railway facilities in the inner suburban boroughs in south-east London .... A new tube railway in this area, possibly via Bricklayers Arms and Peckham to the Crystal Palace .... might well be noted for further study in connection with any long term plan.[1]

*

The fact that Crystal Palace was considered to be a suitable location for a tube railway indicates that the planning authorities were still confident that the Crystal Palace grounds would be redeveloped in order to attract large numbers of visitors. In fact the first length of the proposed tube railway, from the Elephant and Castle on the Bakerloo line to Camberwell Green, was actually started in January 1950, when five shafts were sunk in order to allow tunnelling work. The scheme was scheduled for completion in 1953 at an estimated cost of £4.5 million. However, in September 1950 construction work was suddenly abandoned and it was announced that 'with regret it has been found necessary to defer the proposed extension.'[2]

Shortly after the publication of the long term plan for London's transport system, a scheme was put forward by the National Union of Students to use the Crystal Palace as a national youth sporting and holiday centre with a view to organising the 1951 International Student Games on the site as part of the Festival of Britain celebrations. This idea was turned down by the trustees, who were still hoping that the Government would in some way assist in a restoration project. Two of the trustees of the Crystal Palace, Lord Aberdeen and Lord Ammon, sent letters to *The Times* newspaper about this matter. After deploring the decision to stage the Festival of Britain on the south bank of the Thames instead of siting it at the Crystal Palace, they pointed out that:

*

... it seems that the entire south bank scheme will involve expenditure of something like £10 million, but for very considerably less than this the Crystal Palace could have been rebuilt, not only to house the 1951 Festival of Britain, but to provide a permanent home for the British Industrial Fair .... throughout the remainder of each year the Crystal Palace could have been maintained as an educational and entertainment centre providing the social amenities so badly needed in London .... I join Lord Ammon in the hope that the Government may yet find opportunity to assist the trustees in restoring this national asset as a place for education and recreation and for the promotion of industry, commerce and art.[3]

*

Meanwhile the High Level line continued to be operated in its dilapidated state and passenger numbers remained low. An observer visiting Upper Sydenham station at this time

❧
Plate 80 - The entrance to the coal yard at Honor Oak and a view of the northern elevation of the signal box. There appears to be no signalling for the crossover.
Lens of Sutton Association

Plate 81 - The signal box at Lordship Lane in 1954, which had not been in use since 1924, probably the time that the single siding was removed. The transition from wooden platform to the extension is quite clear.   *Lens of Sutton Association*

noted that when an up train called at the station, no passengers either left or joined it. The porter did not bother to go down to the platform, but waved 'right away' from the footbridge.[4] The changeover from the Southern to British Railways had no noticeable effect upon the working of the line, except that cheap day tickets to London were advertised by British Railways from all local stations. The cost of a 3rd class return fare from the Crystal Palace High Level station to London was set at 1/6d, and this fare was available on weekdays by all trains after 9.30am, and on Sundays and Bank Holidays at all times. Passengers could not return on weekdays between 4.30pm and 6.30pm or between 12 noon and 1.30pm on Saturdays.[5]

In July 1952 Mr Robert Jenkins MP received a letter from one of his Sydenham Hill constituents. Responding to a rumour concerning the possible closure of the High Level line, the constituent pointed out that the line between Nunhead and the Crystal Palace was the only transport link to the City for residents of Sydenham Hill, Wood Vale and the surrounding area. The constituent also noted that although the fares were a little higher than equivalent bus routes, the rail service was quicker. In view of this it was suggested that two-car diesel sets should be employed on the line, with conductors collecting fares. This would dispense with the need for station staff and would allow additional carriages to be used on the busier lines of the Southern Region. A further suggestion was that a 'halt' should be provided on the line at Brenchley Gardens, One Tree Hill, in order to serve the nearby London County Council estates.

However, when Mr Jenkins submitted these suggestions to the Railway Executive he was informed that diesel cars would be uneconomic to run, and that the Brenchley Gardens 'halt'

was unnecessary because residents in that area used Crofton Park station on the Catford Loop. Mr Jenkins also asked the British Transport Commission if the closure rumours had any foundation, and the reply from Lord Hurcomb confirmed that:

*

Crystal Palace High Level branch is under consideration for closure but further information is awaited from the London County Council on their plans for the development of the Crystal Palace site, so it is not yet possible to say what our recommendation will be.

*

Lord Hurcomb also noted that if and when the case was submitted to the Transport Users' Consultative Committee, Mr Jenkins would be allowed to object if he so desired.[6]

In 1953 meetings began to be held on the new car racing track at the Crystal Palace, and these meetings attracted huge crowds:

*

The first meeting was on Whit-Monday 1953, when it was estimated that the attendance was around 50,000. Of these about 8,000 used Low Level and 1,250 High Level, the greatest number of travellers to either station for nearly twenty years.[7]

*

But 1953 was also the year in which further rumours about the closure of the High Level line began to surface. At a July meeting of the Penge and Anerley Ratepayers and Residents Association, held at the Thicket Hotel, the question of a possible permanent closure of the Crystal Palace High Level station was raised. This station served many local residents with its direct run to the City, and the return of the rumour that it was to close was worrying them. Councillor C. Jones told those present that 'We should find out and let people know what is happening, and safeguard the interests of the public in this part of the district'. However, when a newspaper reporter from the *Norwood News* tried to obtain further information, a transport spokesman said that the matter was still under consideration.[8]

The public was not made aware of the fact that a comprehensive document, recommending closure of the High Level line, had been prepared in August 1952 by the Southern Region Branch Lines Committee. (*See Appendix 1*) The Committee estimated that if their recommendations were adopted the net savings to British Rail would be £62,885. It was also pointed out that if former rail passengers utilised the nearby buses and trams, the net improvement to British Transport Commission revenue would be £76,885.

These closure papers were eventually made available to local authorities in the Crystal Palace area, and in January 1954 a local newspaper revealed that Penge Council had been asked to ensure that the report which British Railways had provided be kept confidential, as a close watch was still being kept on the number of passengers using the High Level station.[9]

By March 1954, however, it was known that the closure proposals had been submitted to the Transport Users' Consultative Committee, and a statement was put out by British Railways clarifying the situation.

∗

Proposals are in hand by British Railways to close the Crystal Palace High Level Branch which runs from Nunhead to the Crystal Palace, as the recent volume of

traffic in recent years has been very small. No definite date has been agreed as to when the passenger and freight services will be withdrawn as the matter has still to be considered by the Transport Users' Consultative Committee for London. It is unlikely, however, that the line will be closed before the end of summer. A Railways' spokesman added, 'We want to close it, since the amount of people who use it is negligible.'

∗

A reporter from the *Norwood News* visited the High Level station and wrote

∗

... the descent by stone steps, well worn in the past , must be something like the approach to Tutankamen's Tomb .... All was quiet, except for water dripping from above onto the roof of a waiting train. There were two other passenger trains standing at the platforms which provide accommodation for four. In the distance a cleaner was at work. Otherwise no human being could be seen.[10]

∗

Although dilapidated, the station was of considerable architectural significance. It had cost £100,000 to construct in 1865, and when completed the building received a favourable review in the *Illustrated London News* at that time. When the news of its possible closure became widely known, it was assumed that it would be utilised for some other purpose, and accordingly the firm of Ewart Watson Exhibitions (London) Ltd wrote to British Railways offering to rent the station annually in order to stage the South London (Ideal Home) Exhibition, but the offer was not accepted.[11] The High Level station was

Plate 82 - Less than a year before closure, on 3rd October 1953, this is Crystal Palace High Level looking past a very dilapidated signal box towards Paxton tunnel. Coal wagons and Set 901 can be seen in the sidings and a 4-SUB set has emerged from tunnel.   *Denis Cullum*

Plate 83 - Interior of the High Level station with train awaiting departure from Platform 1. It is August 1954, just a few weeks before closure and ferns are thriving thanks to the water that is able to enter through the broken roof panels.   *Pamlin Prints*

also considered to be a possible site for the British Transport Commission's museum. In July 1954 the Chief Administrative Officer of the Commission confirmed that the subject had been given consideration and had not been definitely ruled out, particularly as rail access would not be required. This would have been an appropriate use for the building but the scheme was never implemented.[12]

March 1954 was also the month in which the Transport Users' Consultative Committee received views on the closure proposals from local authorities and other interested parties. The Upper Norwood Chamber of Commerce informed the Committee that there was no objection to the closure as the economic circumstances appeared to fully justify it. But this view was not shared by any of the local authorities who responded. Penge Council was opposed to closure:

*

The Council respectfully submit that with all the development proposals in hand for housing, sports grounds, cultural amenities and the like, and the need of travellers for a direct service to the City, every effort should be made to keep the branch open for the benefit of the general public.[13]

*

A similar response was given by Lewisham Council:

*

The Memorandum of the Railway Authorities on the operating circumstances of the branch has been given full consideration, and I am now directed to inform you that this Council views the proposal with disfavour, particularly in view of the already inadequate travelling facilities in the Forest Hill district, and that closure of this branch line will accentuate the inconvenience suffered by residents in this area.[14]

*

Camberwell Council was concerned that a decision had been taken before proper consideration had been given to the observations which it had submitted. However, it considered

that no useful purpose could be served by making further representations to the Transport Users' Consultative Committee regarding closure in view of the savings that closure would give British Railways.[15] The Council did, however, receive a letter from a Streatham resident suggesting that if the line were to be closed it could be used for a new arterial road. This idea was forwarded to the British Transport Commission, but in view of the natural difficulties, ie. width of railway, existence of cuttings and the prohibitive expenditure, it was not considered to be practicable.[16]

Prior to a meeting being held to discuss the case for closing the High Level line, the Transport Users' Consultative Committee received a petition from seven local residents. In opposing the closure they suggested that more publicity should be given to the line and that fares should be lowered. They also pointed out that more activities were taking place at the Crystal Palace which would increase passenger numbers, and that new flats and houses were constantly being built in the area. The petition also raised queries about the published closure papers:

*

Whilst we naturally do not challenge the accuracy of the Commission's figures we would be glad to know how the totals of £75,000 and £14,000 given as the annual running costs and takings on the line are arrived at, and whether these totals apply only to the four stations between Nunhead and Crystal Palace.[17] (*See Appendix 1*)

*

The meeting of the Transport Users' Consultative Committee was held in Westminster on 10th June 1954 with representatives of the British Transport Commission on hand to answer questions. A deputation led by Mr H. W. Eames, and including Miss Hester Green, secretary of the 'Save the Crystal Palace Line' committee were allowed to put forward their views, and the Commission also considered communications from the boroughs of Camberwell, Lewisham and Penge, and from the Upper Norwood Chamber of Commerce.

After the deputation had left, a Consultative Committee

spokesman stated that in view of the very poor use of the line, which was being run at a very heavy annual loss, and the alternative bus and rail facilities available to residents in the area after the line was closed, the Committee decided that there was no justification for keeping it open. The spokesman also confirmed that the British Transport Commission was proposing to withdraw both passenger and freight services, and that appropriate arrangements would be made for dealing with local coal traffic. The cost of keeping the line open was given as more than £100,000 a year.[18]

At the end of the meeting the date set for the closure of the Crystal Palace High Level railway was given as Monday, 20th September 1954. The British Transport Commission conveyed this information to the Chief Officer of the Southern Region by means of the following memorandum, dated 29th July 1954:

✻

Arrangements are being made to withdraw passenger services and goods train services on and from Monday 20th September next. It will temporarily be necessary to run empty trains to and from Crystal Palace (HL) for berthing until alternative berthing sidings are available, and to retain one track for emergency access to Upper Sydenham sub-station until superseded in the change of frequency scheme.[19]

✻

Coincidentally the Transport Users' Consultative Committee for London agreed to the closure of the Crystal Palace High Level branch railway on the day before the centenary of the opening of the Crystal Palace at Sydenham by Queen Victoria.[20]

The End of the Line

News of the closure of the Crystal Palace High Level branch appeared in the local press in July 1954 when it was stated that all stations on the Crystal Place High Level branch would close on Monday, 20th September 1954. Passengers were advised to use alternative rail services from Honor Oak Park, Forest Hill, Sydenham Hill, Crystal Palace Low Level and Gipsy Hill stations. The local press also published details of the bus services in the area:

✻

On and from September 15th, London Transport bus service 63 will be extended from the present terminus at Honor Oak to Crystal Palace Parade, serving Lordship Lane and Upper Sydenham. Bus routes 2, 3, 12, 176, and 185 also serve the area with through services to Victoria, West End and the City. Buses also provide connections to Peckham Rye, Denmark Hill, East Dulwich, West Norwood, and Herne Hill stations.[21]

✻

The proposed closure provoked immediate criticism. The *Norwood News* printed an article complaining about the lack of progress in developing the Crystal Place site, and lamented the closure of the High Level branch, '... and as for the bungle of the High Level to Nunhead branch closing just when the district is being developed with vast building schemes - well ! .... and to think people get paid for this sort of thing!' [22] The

issue was also raised in Parliament by Mr Henry Price, MP for Lewisham West. He criticised both the closing of the line, and the procedure by which it was done.

✻

Mr Price said the history of the closing made nonsense of the procedure in which the question is examined by consultative committees. "It demonstrates it as farcical, and in my view, shows that it is merely a façade to impress the gullible that the interests of the consumers are protected," he said. "The interests of the consumers have no chance whatever. When the railways were nationalised one of the arguments strenuously advanced in favour of it was that the element of profitability would be removed and the most important principle would be that of service to the public. It is clear that in the case of the Crystal Palace to Nunhead branch line the reverse has been adopted. It is the element of profitability that matters and the element of public service has been ignored."

Mr Price said there had been no attempt since the war to make this line a commercial proposition. "All the evidence appears to prove that there has been a deliberate attempt on the part of those responsible to depress the value of this line and to make it as unattractive as possible to the public. The Crystal Palace High Level is in the same condition as it was after the war, with a glass roof open to the elements and showing many other signs of dereliction. The station is typical of the line in that it has been allowed almost to rot."

Mr Price said no attempt had been made to advertise the facilities which this line offers. "Perhaps I ought to apologise for a slight exaggeration here. There is one advertisement. Outside one station there is a notice in, I think, these words 'This station is closed on Sundays.'" He added that, as far as he knew, that was the only advertisement on any of the stations concerned. "It is hardly surprising that an unhappy fate has befallen this line financially."

He suggested that instead of the policy, "This line does not pay, let us close it," there should be the policy, "This line is not fully used. Let us see what we can do to popularise it and thus relieve the load on the overburdened road transport system of London. Especially should that be so in this case, where there is a substantial housing development being carried out by the borough councils and the county council. This will have the effect of increasing very substantially the number of potential customers for this railway within the next year or two. Surely that is a peculiar way of giving unbiased and objective consideration, as they should have done in this case."

Mr Price said that he understood that the Committee were there to protect the transport users, but one might be forgiven for imagining that in this case they were there to serve the interests of British Railways and London Transport. There were quotations by Mr Price from correspondence in which Camberwell Council said they felt justified in protesting strongly at the manner in which the matter had been dealt with; from Lewisham Council

Plate 84 - It is the last day of service - 18th September 1954 - but the demolition appears to have started already. This is Platforms 3 and 4 out of use. In spite of this, the real process of demolition did not start until 1956.   *Mile Post 92½ Picture Library; A W V Mace*

who "viewed the proposal with disfavour, particularly in view of the already inadequate travelling facilities in the Forest Hill district." Penge Council said that every effort should be made to keep the line open to meet the growing need because of development of housing, sports grounds, cultural amenities and the existing need for direct rail service to the City. "Every effort should be made to keep the branch open for the benefit of the general public." [23]

∗

These arguments, however, fell on deaf ears. In reply to Mr Price the Joint Parliamentary Secretary, Mr Hugh Molson, said

∗

In the case of these unremunerative lines in London, where there are so many other means of transport, it is those residents of London who have not used the lines while they were available, who are to blame if they now find that they are being closed down. I would remind Mr Price, when he talks about profitability, that one of the principles of the Nationalisation Act was that the British Transport Commission is expected to ensure that, taking one year with another, it covers its expenses.

∗

He added that one of the essentials of effective and up-to-date administration is to close down lines which are no longer remunerative.[24]

When the closure of the High Level line was announced, the coal merchants who had been based at the sidings of the High Level station moved off to Gipsy Hill station on the Low Level line.[25] On Saturday, 18th September 1954 the last electric train from Crystal Palace High Level station left at 11.36pm. Of the

thirty passengers who travelled on this train not more than ten were ordinary passengers; the remainder were members of the Tramways and Railways Society, the Light Railway Transport League, the Talyllyn Railway Preservation Society, the Railway Correspondence and Travel Society, the 1858 (Chessington) Group and the Southern Counties Touring Society. As the train departed the staff, who were due to be transferred to other stations on the following Monday, watched from the top of the staircase.[26]

The 11.36pm train from Crystal Palace High Level station arrived at Nunhead station and switched lines before coming to a halt, watched by crowds of people who were gathered on the platform. The train was now to become the 11.54pm to the Crystal Palace, and would be the last official train to run on the High Level line. Two flags and a board with the letters 'Last Train' were attached to the front by Mr Vivian Orchard and Mr William Henry, of the Railway Enthusiasts Club, Farnborough. This club was always represented on any last train to run on a line which was to be closed down. The flags and board had been used twice before when last trains ran on the Freshwater branch line on the Isle of Wight and on the Gosport to Fareham branch line in Hampshire. Amongst the passengers who were to travel on the last train were Alderman G. Burden, Leader of Camberwell Council, and his wife, Councillor Mrs S. Burden. Alderman Burden had not travelled on the line previously, but his Council had an interest in the railway land as there were plans to utilise some of it for new housing.

The train hooted as it passed Nunhead signal box, Honor Oak, Lordship Lane and Upper Sydenham stations. When the train arrived at the Crystal Palace High Level the remaining passengers posed for photographs with the railwaymen; driver Robert Haywood, who had been driving trains on the Crystal Palace line for seven years, guard Edward Brown, a guard on the line for five years, and porter John Boss, who had been at Crystal Palace station for eight years. Some passengers had their expired season tickets autographed by railway staff and then handed back as souvenirs. The board and the flags were then removed, guard Brown said to porter Boss, *'That's the lot, John,'* and the train then moved off empty into the night to return to Blackfriars. The Palace line was closed.[27]

The last official train was not, however, the last train to run on the High Level line. A 47-year-old bachelor, Mr George Lockie, who had once worked in Canada for the Canadian Pacific Railroad, chartered a special train with seating capacity for 424 people and a buffet car. The steam-hauled train was to be called the 'Palace Centenarian', [28] and was to be hauled by two ex-SE&CR Class C 0-6-0s, Nos.31576 and 31719.[29] There were to be 12 main line carriages attached to these engines and the price of a ticket for this last excursion was set at six shillings.[30]

On Sunday, 19th September 1954 the 'Palace Centenarian' left the High Level station, accompanied by sustained whistling and cheering. The train celebrated the 100 years of service that the Crystal Palace railways had given since the opening of the Crystal Palace in 1854. It carried 550 passengers including members of Upper Norwood Chamber of Commerce, who had a reserved compartment and were issued with a perpetual pass to the buffet car. All travellers were given a souvenir ticket bearing the legend '1854-1954 Palace Centenarian Special - Guaranteed Excursion. Last steam train on the Crystal Palace (High Level) Branch. 19th September 1954'.

The 'Palace Centenarian' passed along the High Level line and at Honor Oak it was met by an elderly 'official' dressed in top hat and frock coat, the stationmaster uniform of a century ago. The train then continued on a journey around the lines of South London.

*

... to Peckham, and on past Battersea Goods Yard to Richmond. Then by Kingston, Clapham Junction, Herne Hill, Tulse Hill, West Norwood and Gipsy Hill to Crystal Palace Low Level, and on through Sydenham to London Bridge, and later Blackfriars. Directions were altered and the engine tugged the cheering crowds back through Denmark Hill .... and so to the High Level again.[31]

*

The driver of this last steam train was Sid Wanstall, forty years a railwayman. When interviewed he said, 'I remember when we took most of the Cup Final crowds to the Crystal Palace ground long before Wembley.' His fireman was Donald Everest, whose main concern was the preservation of the engine. 'As long as they don't melt the old engine down. Sixty years old, and going like a young un.'[32]

The Wainwright Class C 0-6-0 locomotive had for many years hauled a daily freight service of mainly domestic fuel from Herne Hill yard to the High Level sidings.[33] Built between 1900 to 1908, the engines were popular amongst the footplate men.

*

The footplate provided a neat and spacious area which afforded a long wooden box down one side to enable the crew to place their belongings inside. It also served as a comfortable seat for the fireman between firing. The

Plate 85 - The 'Palace Centenarian' approaching Crystal Palace High Level on 19th September 1954, the day after public closure. The train was worked by Class C 0-6-0s Nos.31576 and 31719.   *R C Riley; The Transport Treasury*

Plate 86 - With the DC power off, one hopes, the 'Palace Centenarian' is about to leave Crystal Palace High Level on 19th September 1954. A window in the subway that led under The Parade to the Crystal Palace can be seen to the left of the plume of steam.

R C Riley; The Transport Treasury

firegrate was flat, and so it was not the policy to bank the fire high up under the fire hole door. An even spread, well alight, preserved the 160lb steam pressure very nicely.[34]

*

When *The Times* newspaper reported the closure of the High Level line, it noted that the planning officers of nearby local authorities were interested in redeveloping the railway land which would become available when the track and the intermediate stations were removed. Camberwell, Lewisham and Deptford Councils had obviously considered various options. The site of the High Level station, being the largest area of land, could be used for new housing, whilst the ribbon of double track running for three and three-quarter miles to Nunhead could become public open space. They also considered that the 430 yard long Paxton tunnel could have a future use as a civil defence shelter, or as a store.[35] However, before any redevelopment could be undertaken, it was necessary to demolish the High Level station and lift the track, work which did not commence until 1956. Meanwhile, in November 1954 a short article appeared in the local press backing the decision to close the High Level line.

*

Somehow it seems that British Railways were right. Now that the High Level station is closed and the 63 bus service has been introduced there are but few passengers. True it is a sparse 16 minute service, which means a long dreary wait in Sydenham Hill on a rainy day, but when at last a bus does come it is not carrying a payload. In time it may pay, meanwhile London Transport is providing a public service without thought of profit. We must give them their due.[36]

*

But the general opinion about the closure was that it had

been carried out in error. As late as 1968 the matter was still under discussion in the press.

*

It is the curse of Norwood ! They took away our perfectly good railway line when it was clear to the dimmest mind that it would have become an increasing asset as suburban traffic expanded, and pushed the traffic onto the roads where it is least wanted .... Both the Norwood Society and the Upper Norwood Chamber of Commerce have urged the Greater London Council to open part of the High Level site as a temporary car park to relieve congestion.[37]

*

The lifting of the track eventually got under way, but in March 1957 a most surprising headline appeared in the *Advertiser*

*

THE GREAT RAILWAY MIX-UP ! Mystery move to save Palace line even as stations are torn down.

*

The newspaper stated that there were plans to save the line in order to serve the new LCC sports centre to be built at the Crystal Palace. The battle to save the line was revealed by Mr Martin Jenkins, LCC member for Dulwich, at a conference held at Camberwell Town Hall. He said:

*

This is a matter of extreme gravity. Particularly as within three or four years Crystal Palace is going to be transformed into a national, indeed an international sports centre, attracting up to 10,000 or 20,000 people a night to that part of London. All of us have been consistently urging the need to improve transport facilities. I am engaged with others in working very hard to prevent the Crystal Palace line being built on. I feel certain that when Crystal Palace becomes the sports centre the authorities will look round in despair for greatly improved transport services. If we can keep the land unbuilt until the Crystal Palace is developed I believe we shall get the line back.

*

However, the LCC were at the time negotiating with the British Transport Commission to buy the land on behalf of Camberwell, Deptford and Lewisham Councils, who wanted the land for housing development. Camberwell Council had, in fact, called upon the MP for Dulwich, Mr Robert Jenkins, to press for a speeding up of the negotiations. Mr Jenkins stated that he was unaware of any plans to save the line.

*

The move that Mr Stevens mentioned has come as a complete surprise to me. I have consistently opposed the closing of the Crystal Palace line. I think it ought never to have been closed. But once it was and there was no question of it being reopened I went all out for the land to be utilised for housing or any other purpose in the public interest. I did not want it to stand derelict.[38]

*

This argument obviously won the day, for no further action was taken to save the line.

The lifting of the track, which commenced in 1956, was accompanied by the demolition of both Honor Oak and Lordship Lane stations, and the removal of Forest Hill bridge and Lordship Lane bridge. The station house at Upper Sydenham station was, however, left intact because of its hillside location in Wells Road. Prior to the track being removed from the steep embankment outside Nunhead station, the Transport Commission received complaints from residents of houses in Ivydale Road and Athenlay Road. These houses backed onto the line and were the constant target of stone throwing hooligans who ventured onto the track. Trouble was also encountered on the section of line which ran on an embankment up to the Forest Hill Road bridge. At this point a 10ft deep landslide occurred, the spoil falling into the gardens of houses in Marmora Road. Once again the Transport Commission received complaints from residents who wished to obtain compensation for their buried plants and uprooted trees.[39]

The High Level line had been bought by the LCC for the sum of £35,000, and as a result of this the five-acre site which had been Honor Oak station was allocated to Lewisham Council for housing. Similarly, the site of the former Lordship Lane station was allocated to Camberwell Council who had plans to construct a housing estate adjacent to the Sydenham Hill Estate.[40] However, no decision about the 10-acre site at Crystal Palace High Level could be taken until the huge High Level station had been demolished, which was not started until 1961.

The Crystal Palace High Level station was briefly used in 1958 by the film director Ken Russell when it became the location for one of his earliest films, 'Amelia and the Angel'.[41] When demolition eventually commenced, the red brick towers of the High Level station were the first structures to be demolished. The *Norwood News* reported that:

*

While demolition work has been in progress hundreds of pigeon nests filled with eggs have been found. Nearby residents have been helping the workmen find homes for the eggs, which are still warm, and looking after the baby birds which have broken through.

One of the surprising features of the towers was that they were hollow. "I dropped a brick through the rotten floor of one of them" (said Mr Lynch in charge of demolition) "and it plunged right down through 50ft of brickwork to the ground." The great piles of bricks will be used for building in the sports centre.[42]

*

Because of the demolition work the station had to be barricaded against trespassers, as it was an obvious danger spot. Men were also employed to guard the premises.[43] Fortunately the ornamental subway which had conveyed 1st class passengers into the Crystal Palace was left intact, enabling future generations to marvel at its octagonal columns and vaulted ornamental red and white brick roof.

When demolition of the station had been completed, prefabs were temporarily placed on the site. In 1967 the Norwood Society requested the MP for Dulwich, Mr Sam Silkin, to press the GLC to undertake development of the High Level site, and to ensure that this was carried out as 'part of coherent re-planning for the whole Crystal Palace area'.[44] Local traders in the Norwood Triangle considered that the best use of the site would be to develop it as a car park; however, the GLC did not agree with this suggestion.[45] The site therefore remained undeveloped, and in 1976 the Farquhar Road bridge, which

Plate 87 - It certainly went the distance! Honor Oak Down distant on 17th September 1954, the day before official closure of the line. The signal was originally installed by the LC&DR.   *Denis Cullum*

crossed the Crystal Palace High Level station site, was found to be in need of urgent repairs and was therefore temporarily closed. It was necessary to strengthen the bridge deck and abutments and renew the parapets, so that the bridge could be used for site access during construction work on a new housing scheme which was scheduled to commence in 1978.[46]

This was not the first time that the Farquhar Road bridge had caused problems. Some twenty years earlier the bridge had been closed to traffic when a police officer noticed a depression in the footway near to the junction with Crystal Palace Parade. On closer inspection it was found that material from the roof of the tunnel had fallen onto the railway line. When excavation work was carried out, the workmen found that at a depth of three feet they were able to see through the roof of the tunnel to the rails 50ft below.[47] In addition to the houses which were eventually constructed, a residential nursing home was built on the site of the High Level station. The home was built despite opposition from King's Community Health Council, who considered that the site was too remote.

The two disused railway tunnels on the High Level line were sealed at each end with iron gates to prevent children from gaining access. Usage of the Paxton Tunnel at the Crystal Palace, however, was considered in 1973 by both Southwark Council and the Dulwich Estates Governors, under some of whose land it passed. The tunnel was found to have bricks and debris falling from the roof, and it was therefore considered necessary to conduct an urgent investigation into its condition, as it ran beneath private houses and several roads. Although the Council owned the tunnel, the governors agreed to pay the sum of £800 towards the £2,500 required for an investigation of its structural condition.

This work was subsequently carried out by Sir Frederick Snow and Partners. Camberwell Council assured the public that the tunnel was not about to collapse, and on completion of investigatory work the tunnel was used for the storage of materials. Although the press noted that it had been frivolously suggested that it could become an underground night club known as 'The Tunnel'.[48]

In 1977 memories of Lordship Lane station were briefly revived when *The Times* newspaper published a story about one of the paintings by the French Impressionist Camille Pissaro. This painting, showing a train departing from what was believed to be Penge station, was on display in the Courtauld Institute Galleries at the University of London. However, after several visitors to the gallery had expressed doubt as to whether the station shown was indeed Penge, the curator wrote to the *Railway Magazine*, which in turn invited comments from its readers.

✳

The magazine's readers took up the challenge and in this month's issue came the answer from Mr B. L. Halford of Tonbridge, who pointed out that it could not possibly be Penge West because the line through that station was quadrupled 24 years before Pissaro set up his easel. Mr Troutman (curator of the Courtauld Institute) suggested that the picture might have been painted from a bridge over the track, but again the evidence is damning; Penge West is bridgeless. Mr Halford wrote: "I have considered other stations in the locality and have now positively identified it as Lordship Lane station which was closed in 1954. The painting is of a view from Cox's Walk footbridge, looking north towards Nunhead, and the train is travelling towards Crystal Palace terminus. The branch was opened in 1865, and, as little undergrowth has appeared along the earthworks illustrated, a date of 1871 appears to agree."[49]

✳

What is left of the High Level line today? Although new houses have been built across the tracks in some places, it is possible to follow a green walk to the former Crystal Palace station, through an area which in some parts still appears almost rural. This five-mile walk has been promoted by the Friends of The Great North Wood, and leads from Nunhead station via Camberwell Old Cemetery and the Dulwich Wood House tavern, to Crystal Palace station. The old railway line still maintains a presence; Cox's Walk footbridge from where Pissaro painted Lordship Lane station is still intact, as are the two tunnels which served

Plate 88 - A somewhat murky day in 1956 with tracklifting well under way at Crystal Palace High Level. *Lens of Sutton Association*

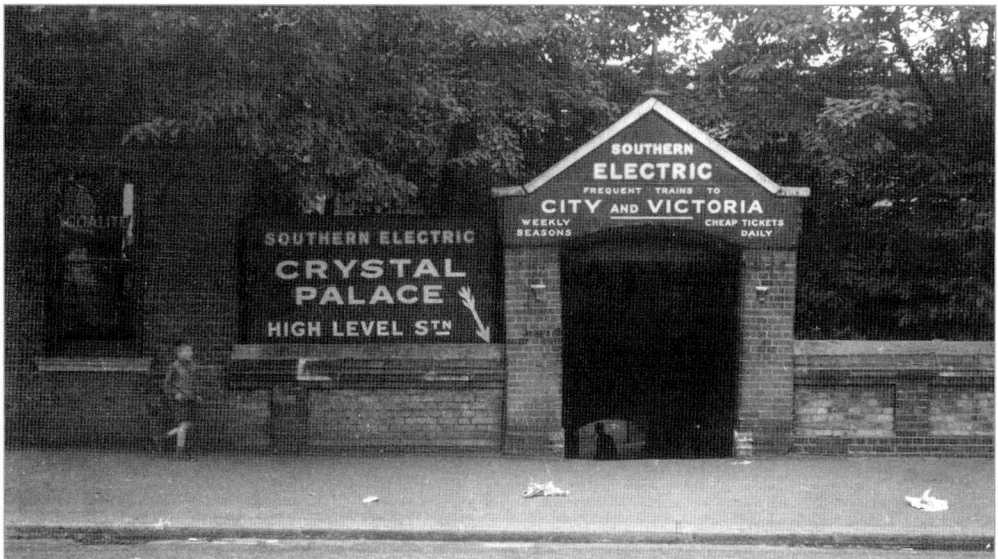

Plate 89 - The side entrance opening onto Crystal Palace Parade, 18th September 1954. 'Coalite' is written on the window just behind the boy but whether the coal merchant was still operating at that time is not known.

Mile Post 92½ Picture Libary;
A W V Mace

the line. The station house at Upper Sydenham still stands in Wells Road, and the long ornate wall at Crystal Palace, into which is set the ornamental subway, can still be seen.[50]

LAST WORDS

The High Level branch line gave 90 years of service, although it was rarely profitable. In fact anybody taking a fleeting look at the history of the line would probably come to the conclusion that its closure was inevitable. Passenger traffic was negligible after the destruction of the Crystal Palace, and World War II left the line in a decrepit state, with much of the electric cabling in need of replacement. In addition, the High Level station was left in a near state of dereliction and other stations on the line were badly in need of repair.

The haphazard development of the suburban railway system in London led to competition between the railway companies, and this in turn led to duplication of railway lines. Consequently, throughout its life the High Level line had to compete with stations on the rival Crystal Palace Low Level line which was originally constructed by the London, Brighton & South Coast Railway. This situation would not have been so bad if the High Level line could also have served other areas, in fact the future of the line would have been assured. However, in the 19th century, repeated attempts to expand the High Level route beyond the Crystal Palace proved to be unsuccessful, and it remained a branch line throughout its existence.

High fares were a constant source of complaint on the High Level railway, and it is difficult to understand why such a policy was adopted by every railway company that took control of the line. Both passengers, and successive General Managers of the Crystal Palace, protested strongly about the high fares, and there is little doubt that the fares strategy resulted in a significant loss of traffic over the years. It is important to note in this respect that the spread of bus and tram services in the early part of the 20th century also caused the railway company to lose both passengers and revenue. Trams were particularly successful as the London County Council adopted a low fares policy. It should also be noted that because the High Level railway was

left in such a state of dereliction after the war, many passengers would have been deterred from using this railway, particularly as it was possible to utilise other cheaper and more visually pleasing forms of transportation.

Despite the facts given above, the decision to close the Crystal Palace High Level railway remains contentious. Firstly, there were several missed opportunities to operate the line profitably. The introduction of diesel railbuses on some railways in the 1930s proved conclusively that railbuses could operate at least 30% cheaper than steam hauled trains. Subsequent development of railbuses led to the introduction of diesel multiple units. These were larger and faster vehicles which were capable of providing fast services and handling heavier traffic.[51] The introduction of railbuses on the High Level line could have made its uneconomic service economically viable. However, there was never any attempt to utilise this type of passenger vehicle on the Crystal Palace services; in fact the Railway Executive, when asked to comment on a suggestion to use two-car sets on the line, said that it would be uneconomic to use diesel cars on electrified lines.[52]

A further lost opportunity concerned the extension of the tube railway to Crystal Palace. Various schemes were put forward over the years to extend the Bakerloo tube line, firstly to Camberwell Green and then on to the Crystal Palace. However, despite repeated requests from Camberwell, Deptford and Lambeth Councils for improved transport facilities in South London, none of the tube schemes was ever completed. Even in the early part of the 21st century the only access to the tube for residents of south-east London is via the East London line at New Cross, or by the Docklands Light Railway. It would have been relatively easy to convert the High Level branch line to a tube railway, and this may even have brought about the birth of a new Crystal Palace. 'Ironically, new talk of another Palace was finally shelved in favour of the National Sports Centre ..... sited nearer the remaining Low Level station, on the grounds that High Level transport facilities were insufficient!!'[53] It is sad to note that the closure papers for the line show that the tube option was considered, (*App.1: 9c*) but the decision was taken not to take previous discussions on the matter into account.

The closure of the High Level branch was also a missed opportunity to cater for new housing development which was taking place in the vicinity of the line. When first constructed the line served mainly areas with low population densities. Large villas occupied much of the area around Sydenham and consequently passenger traffic on the line was light. However, the railways had enabled the middle classes to live in the suburbs whilst being able to commute to work in the City, and by the 1950s new estates were being built with much higher densities of population. Had the High Level line been kept open for a few more years, it is likely that passenger traffic would have increased considerably, thus enabling the line to become profitable. The closure papers (*App.1: 9b*) refer to housing development in the area, but dismiss this as a reason for keeping the line open.

Within the closure papers there is also a surprising statement about the possible long term development of the Crystal Palace site:

∗

(Closure Details) Recently passed to the London County Council - Plans for some development but only of a minor nature - unlikely to develop much additional traffic - therefore no case for retention of the line on this account.[54]

∗

However, as late as 1950 the LCC had considered taking over the Crystal Palace site with the intention of spending over £100,000 on renovation work. This was to be undertaken with a view to restoring it to '... the playground of Londoners which it was before the disastrous fire of 1936'. The LCC considered that the site could be utilised as a recreation and sports centre serving South London, at which national and international events could also be held. It was considered that:

∗

The fire has given an opportunity for providing a group of buildings and a layout of outstanding architectural and planning interest ... The site is admirably suited to this purpose, and we suggest that its potentialities as an amusement, exhibition, recreation and sports centre should be exploited to the full.

∗

With regard to the reconstruction of the Crystal Palace, the LCC noted that this would be a long term project, but that the price of construction would probably fall significantly before the commencement of building work.[55]

The enthusiasm of the LCC with regard to the future of the Crystal Palace site, coupled with the fact that we now know that a world class sports centre was eventually to be constructed in the Palace grounds, serves to underline how wrong the British Transport Commission was in its assessment of the potential for development of the Crystal Palace site. The assumption made in the closure papers that no new building would ever be constructed there is extraordinary, considering the amount of discussion which had already taken place about its long term future. The British Transport Commission must also have been aware that a competition had been held in 1946 to obtain a design for a new Palace, but the cost had proved to be prohibitive at that time.

In addition to the LCC, in 1950 Lambeth Council also discussed the possibility of restoring the former amenities at Crystal Palace. The Council recognised that any large scale development would involve high priority being given to road improvements which would ultimately be needed in the area, and that the construction cost of a new Crystal Palace would be in excess of £9,000,000. It was therefore decided to temporarily fence off the area until development could be undertaken.[56] As mentioned previously, the abandonment of the High Level line prevented the construction of a new Crystal Palace, and led to the National Sports Centre being located near to the transport facilities offered at the Low Level station. It is certain that a new Crystal Palace would have rejuvenated the area, and certainly would have provided the High Level railway with an ample supply of passengers.

The process for closing branch lines, which was developed following nationalisation in 1948, can also be considered unsatisfactory:

∗

The Transport Users Consultative Committees were supposed to liaise with both the British Transport Commission and transport users; one of their major roles was to judge the merits of closure proposals put forward by the Commission. There was, however, mounting concern that the committees were not always acting in the best interests of the public. It appeared that of 118 closure proposals submitted between 1948 and 1955, the committees had supported the BTC proposals in all but two. There was now a widespread and quite justified belief that the Central Transport Consultative Committee, funded and staffed by the Commission, was not in the slightest degree independent.[57]

∗

Although Parliament considered the consultative process to be satisfactory, repeated complaints about closures eventually resulted in the Parliamentary Secretary to the Minister of Transport having to make a response. 'I want to make it clear that these committees are not "stooges" of the BTC, as some people are inclined sometimes to think or say ...'[58] However, the published statistics for branch line closures showed conclusively that the British Transport Commission was pursuing a firm policy to save money on stretches of line and stations which were not paying their way. From January 1948 until February 1954 over 200 branch lines, with a route mileage of 1,546 miles, had been wholly or partially closed. About 1,000 miles of this total had been closed to passenger traffic only, 300 for freight and 250 for both passenger and freight. In addition, 196 individual stations had been closed for passenger traffic, 75 for freight and 47 for both. The British Railways comment on these statistics was '... remember that pruning is done to promote vigorous growth.'[59] The need for such a drastic closure programme became apparent in 1955, when it was disclosed that the British Transport Commission was in serious financial difficulties, having accumulated a deficit of £70 million. The closures were therefore deemed to be necessary to allow the Commission to eventually pay its way. However, the deficit continued to increase throughout the rest of the decade and the

Plate 90 - The track may be gone but the power lingered on for a while. This sub-station was built as part of the electrification scheme and served both the main line and the Crystal Palace branch. The ventilation shaft to the left carried cables down into the Penge tunnel, which ran below. The Southern Region's Branch Lines Committee recommended that a single, non-electrified line should remain in place to service the sub-station until revised arrangements were in place under the change of frequency scheme.

Lens of Sutton Association

Government was eventually forced to intervene and agree to make a substantial loan to the British Transport Commission.

The railway closure procedure was therefore based primarily upon the need for branch lines to make a profit, and very little account was taken of the need to provide a service. The loss of a railway reduced the employment prospects of local people and restricted the growth of an area. Residents could only commute to work if adequate bus and tram services were available, whilst local businesses often suffered a loss of customers, and were forced to arrange alternative road transport for the supply and delivery of goods and freight. Of course railways could always be re-opened, but in most cases the stations were demolished and the track was lifted and, as in the case of the High Level line, new housing developments were speedily built on the railway land. When these lines were closed it was not appreciated that traffic congestion on roads would become such a major problem. Who could have foreseen at that time that future Government policy would be to encourage people to utilise public transport, and in particular the railways, rather than travel by car?

After the decision to close the High Level line had been taken, it is surprising that the preservation of the High Level station was not considered to be important. The station had considerable architectural merit and had cost £100,000 to construct at 19th century prices. It was not a listed building, but its worth was obviously appreciated by somebody at the British Transport Commission, as it was put forward for possible use as the Commission's museum. It is inconceivable that other uses could not have been found for this impressive structure, for its retention would have certainly proved beneficial to the surrounding area. It can only be assumed that long before the closure details were made public the High Level site had been earmarked for housing development by the local authorities.

Although local people made only limited use of the High Level branch line during its existence, they appear to have woken up to the potential long term damage that its closure would do to those areas served by the line, and their protests were registered accordingly. The British Transport Commission, however, made

its case for closure purely on the economic conditions which prevailed in 1954, and scant consideration was given to any long term development plan for either the Crystal Palace site or the Sydenham area in general. What most local people thought about the closure of the Crystal Palace High Level railway is adequately summed up in this final quotation, taken from *The Phoenix Suburb* by Alan R Warwick:

*

The High Level Railway from Nunhead survived the war, as did the High Level station itself. But this survival did not save the rail link between Norwood and London via the wooded scenery of Sydenham and Lordship Lane. With an utter lack of foresight, or sense of responsibility towards a whole district, but because it was expedient at the moment, the railway connection was uprooted, and the bridges and the fine High Level station erased. With indecent speed, which forestalled any second thoughts for restoring the line in some form, blocks of dwellings were built over the empty track.

One cannot but ask oneself why a London suburb, which had so many times multiplied its population, should no longer need the High Level line, and increasingly so in the future. This was lunatic thinking by authorities who should have known better, and have thought wisely and constructively. Whatever the diminished volume of traffic in those special years shortly after the war - the last train ran on September 19th, 1954 - the massive future potential was there to make maximum use of that track way through a populous area. As it is, the potential has been forced on to overcrowded roads which the authorities themselves insist are inadequate for their purpose.

It is little wonder that residents' societies and local amenity societies have come into being in the last ten or twelve years to protect local interests and to make protest against such high handed encroachment by local government and ministerial bureaucracy.[60]

*

Plate 91 - Wagons in place for the removal of scrap and debris the day after the formal closure of the branch, Sunday, 19th September 1954. The carriage stock for the 'Palace Centenarian' can be seen at another platform. The two wooden wagons are ex-private owner vehicles, both with end-tipping doors. The nearer one is No.P379205, the far one No.P54757. Note the netting strung from the roof in the hope of catching falling debris.

Lens of Sutton Association

Demolition

(Above) Plate 92 - The roof is reduced to a skeleton, revealing the French turrets on one of the northern towers. Some track is still in place to facilitate removal of the debris.

Lens of Sutton Association

Plate 93 - There'll be no coming back from this. The site of the High Level station as it was on 15th April 1961. After final clearance the site was used for residential development.

R C Riley; The Transport Treasury

❀ *Appendix One* ❀

CLOSURE PAPERS

The following details are copied from the closure papers for the Crystal Palace High Level branch line which are currently held at The National Archives (AN 174/71).

SOUTHERN REGION BRANCH LINES COMMITTEE
BRANCH LINES INVESTIGATION
CRYSTAL PALACE (HL) BRANCH

1

LOCATION
From Nunhead on the Catford Loop to Crystal Palace (HL) Terminus.

ROUTE MILEAGE
3 miles 60 chains double track, electrified.

PW CLASSIFICATION
"B" (ii)

STATIONS
Honor Oak, Lordship Lane, Upper Sydenham, Crystal Palace (HL)
There are coal sidings at Honor Oak and Crystal Palace (HL). General freight traffic is not dealt with on the line. Crystal Palace (HL) is used for stock stabling purposes, 16 electric coaches and 24 steam coaches being normally accommodated, only the electric stock being in regular service.

TRAIN SERVICE
Electric services to and from Blackfriars, 44 trains in each direction Monday to Friday, 40 up 37 down Saturdays. First train up 5.46am down 7.1am. Last train up 11.36pm down 12.5am (Crystal Palace timings) No Sunday service. One freight trip in each direction (weekdays only)

2

ANNUAL TRAFFIC RECEIPTS
(based on year 1950 adjusted to 1952 levels)

	LOCAL TO BRANCH	THROUGH FORWARDED	THROUGH RECEIVED	TOTAL
	£	£	£	£
Passengers (Ordinary & Workmen)	1079	6754	1563	9396
Season Tickets	54	7606	95	7755
Parcels	-	79	27	106
Freight	-	-	53	53
Coal, Coke & Patent fuel	-	-	24239	24239
Miscellaneous	61	-	-	61
	1,194	14,439	25,977	41,610

3

PROPOSAL
To close entirely and recover assets, subject to reservation at item 9.

4

ANNUAL ESTIMATED LOSS OF RECEIPTS
Passenger	-	£12,900
Parcels	-	Nil
Freight	-	Nil
		£12,900
Estate Rent etc	-	644
Commercial Advertising	-	260
		£13,824	say £14,000

No extra cartage or other similar costs.

5

ANNUAL REDUCTION IN EXPENDITURE (1952 levels)

Civil Engineer	£	£
Wages and materials	4899	
Repair & Renewal of Bridges	11650	
Renewal of Permanent Way	2748	19297
Mechanical & Electrical Engineer		
Track Equipment - repairs	10	
Track Equipment - renewals	129	139
Signal & Telephone Engineer		
Wages and materials	225	
Renewals	616	841
Train Working		
Freight		
Rolling Stock - Repairs	364	
Rolling Stock - Renewals	122	
Wages	1213	
Fuel etc	1012	2711
Passenger		
97% of total potential savings (see paragraph 9)	22828	25539
Station etc Expenses		
Operating	7469	
Commercial	1349	
Telephones	18	
M & E Engineer (cranes)	18	8854
Estate & Rating Surveyor		18

Annual Reduction in Expenditure (continued)

Interest savings		
Civil Engineer	20588	
Signal & Telephone Engineer	1021	
Estate & Rating Surveyor	2333	
Mechanical & Electrical Engineer - Cranes	24	
Electrification Assets	234	
Rolling Stock (Freight Engine)	270	24470
	Total	£79,285

6
STAFF CHANGES INCLUDED IN ITEM 5

	Posts to be saved	
Civil Engineer		
Ganger	2	
Sub Ganger	2	
Lengthman	8	12
Train Working		
Driver	1	
Fireman	1	
Guard (Goods)	1	3
Station Staff		
Operating Stationmaster (3)	1	
Station Foreman	2	
Signalman (3)	3	
Leading Porter / Signalman (4)	3	
Leading Porter	6	
Porter	3	18
Commercial		
Booking Clerk (5)	2	
Goods Porter	1	3

7
ALTERNATIVE FACILITIES
(Document gives a list of nearby train lines and bus services)

It is thought that while some of the passengers would transfer to alternative train services, the greater number would probably use the bus services - the LTE having seen the detailed train census figures propose, concurrently with the closing of the branch, to extend route 63 (King's Cross - Blackfriars - Elephant & Castle - Peckham - Honor Oak) from Honor Oak to Crystal Palace (HL) along the route of the branch line, serving all the stations concerned. It is considered that this, in conjunction with other road and rail services available, will adequately meet traffic requirements.

Parcels
Can readily be dealt with at surrounding stations.

Freight
Only traffic considered is coal required at Crystal Palace (HL) and Honor Oak. Pen accommodation for the displaced coal merchants can be made available at Penge West, Gipsy Hill and Brockley Lane. It will probably be necessary to remove one existing siding at Penge West and certain expenditure will be incurred.

8
OBJECTIONS ETC
Legal Position - No legal objections to closing.
Staff Consultation - Has taken place in accordance with agreed procedures.
Transport Users' Consultative Committee - Has been advised and consideration is awaited.
Local Authorities, Traders etc - Have been advised in the agreed form.

9
OTHER ITEMS OF IMPORTANCE
Previous Closing
As a wartime measure the passenger service was suspended from May 1944 to March 1946. Owing to poor public support of the Sunday trains after the service was restored, these were withdrawn in October 1948, since when the service has been 'weekdays only'.

Possibility of Increased Traffic
Investigation has not revealed any possibilities of development likely to justify retention of the line except:-

a) Crystal Palace Site
Recently passed to London County Council - Plans for some development but only of a minor nature - unlikely to develop much additional traffic - therefore no case for retention of the line on this account.
b) London County Council and other Housing Developments
London County Council has long term plans for development of an estate between Lordship Lane and Crystal Palace. Matter has been discussed with London County Council and they agreed that the extended 63 bus service would be sufficient, and the High Level line unnecessary.
c) Tube Extension
In the London Working Party Report dated 1949 it was implied that (paragraph 31) a tube line extension might ultimately be extended to connect with this branch near Lordship Lane, but in view of the indefinite position it does not seem that this factor need be taken into account in the present enquiry.

Berthing of Stock
If closed, stock at High Level station could be moved to Bellingham at a cost not exceeding £34,000.

Electric Power Supply
A sub station at Upper Sydenham supplies traction current for the branch, and for the main Kent Coast line via Chatham (which is in tunnel immediately below). If the branch is closed the sub station would be transferred to a site at West Dulwich. The net extra cost of this transfer, debitable against the scheme to close the branch, is estimated at £3,000.

Continuing Liabilities
So long as the sub station continues in operation at Upper Sydenham it will be necessary to provide emergency rail access (as no road approach). This means that a single length of non electrified track will need to be left from Nunhead to the sub station - a distance of approximately 3 miles - for about 5 years. Short term liability for inspection and maintenance about £75 per annum.
It will also be necessary to maintain the two existing 11,000 volt

cables from Nunhead to Upper Sydenham along this line until the sub station is moved. These requirements will not involve any substantial expenditure. The normal 'continuing liability' until the land can be sold is £1,200 per annum.

Heavy Items of Repairs & Renewal in next 10 years

If line is kept open expenditure of approximately £20,000 on platform renewals, work on the roof of High Level station, and general maintenance, must be incurred almost at once. A further £24,000 on permanent way renewal, and £7,000 on general maintenance and repair of war damage would have to be spent within the next 10 years - a total of £51,000. This allows only for limited facilities at Lordship Lane - to rebuild it to its pre-war standard would involve a further £29,000.

Rolling Stock Savings

1 - 'C' Class 0-6-0 tender locomotive.

Train Working Costs

The passenger trains working on this branch run to and from Blackfriars or Holborn Viaduct, and the annual costs are as follows:-

Repairs	-	£1,389
Renewals	-	£2,926
Wages etc	-	£6,323
Fuel etc	-	£12,896
		£23,534

There are 3 four car electric suburban units involved, and 7 motormen, 6 guards and 2 carriage servicemen. While the service is not required on the main line portion (from Nunhead onwards) during the slack hours, it would be necessary to operate during the morning and evening business periods, thus requiring the retention of the electric train units and staff. Closure of the Crystal Palace branch would enable peak hour relief trains to be provided on the Catford Loop line where overcrowding occurs at present, but where it has not hitherto been practicable owing to track occupation between Nunhead and Cambria Junction (Denmark Hill), to effect any improvement.

The service between Nunhead and Blackfriars given by certain Crystal Palace (HL) trains would therefore be maintained, and it is considered equitable to credit the scheme with passenger train working savings apportioned on the basis of mileage actually saved as compared with total mileage. This represents 97%, and the sum of £22,828 has therefore been included in item 5.

Net Result of Proposals

Savings in Expenditure (item **5**)		£79,285
Less Loss of receipts to British Railways (item **4**)		£14,000
		£65,285
Less Stock Berthing scheme		
Repairs & Renewals	£910	
Interest	£1,360	
Interest on cost of sub station on alternative site £120	say:	£2,400
Net savings to British Railways		£62,885
Increased net revenue to LTE road services about		£14,000
Net Improvement in BTC revenue		£76,885

10
Recommendations

That the line be closed and assets recovered, and surplus land sold, subject to a single non-electrified track being retained to give emergency access to Upper Sydenham sub-station until such time as the sub-station is replaced elsewhere under the change of frequency scheme.

D F M Lindsay
Operating Dept

H C Walter
Chairman Commercial Dept

G F George
Civil Engineers Dept

Southern Region Branch Lines Committee
EP/BL 57
August 1952
Revised May 1954

❊ *Appendix Two* ❊

CRYSTAL PALACE & SOUTH LONDON JUNCTION RAILWAY PROSPECTUS

The following prospectus for the Crystal Palace & South London Junction Railway appeared in *The Times* newspaper on the 3rd June 1863:-

CRYSTAL PALACE and
SOUTH LONDON JUNCTION RAILWAY

Extension of the London Chatham and Dover Railway by Peckham to the Crystal Palace. Share capital £675,000; representing 675,000 £10 shares, divided into 33,750 six per cent preference B shares, £10 each, and 33,750 A shares, £10 each. Issue of B preference shares, six per cent dividend.

DIRECTORS
Chairman
Sir Cusack P. Roney, Langham-place, London
    - Director of the London Chatham and Dover Railway
Sir C. H. I. Rich, Bart, Nottingham-place, London
    - Director of the London Chatham and Dover Railway
Edward W. Edwards Esq., Brighton
    - Director of the London Chatham and Dover Railway
Henry Tootal Esq., Cambridge-terrace, Hyde Park
T. Holroyd Esq., Temple, London
Secretary - G. F. Holroyd Esq.
Solicitors - Messrs. Freshfields and Newman, New Bank-buildings
Bankers - Messrs. Barclay, Bevan and Co. Lombard-street
Engineer - F. T. Turner Esq. 15, Parliament-street, Westminster
Auditors - J. Weise Esq., Messrs. Coleman, Turquand, Youngs and Co.; Charles Banks Esq.
Brokers - Messrs Knight, Coleman and Co., 1 Royal Exchange-buildings

Offices - Victoria Station, Pimlico

The Crystal Palace and South London Junction Railway is an extension of the London Chatham and Dover Railway by Peckham to the Crystal Palace. The city and west-end will thus be brought into direct communication with the Crystal Palace, and with the residential district extending along the range of hills between Peckham and Norwood at present unprovided with railway accommodation.

The railway will ascend the hills from Peckham by a gradient far less steep than that of the present line from Sydenham to the Palace.

The station at the Crystal Palace will be on a level with the floor of the building, with several means of access thereto without steps. The great advantage of this must be obvious, when it is borne in mind that by the existing line passengers have to make use of the same access for arrival and departure, to alight at a distance of a quarter of a mile from the building, and to ascend 150 steps.

The line will bring the Palace, and the beautiful residential districts in its vicinity (viz. at Norwood, Upper Sydenham, and Forest-hill.) into communication with the Victoria Station at Pimlico, with the Station of the London Chatham and Dover Railway at Blackfriars, the Finsbury-circus, and numerous other stations on the Metropolitan Railway, besides the populous suburban districts of Clapham, Brixton, Stockwell, Camberwell, Denmark-hill, Newington, Walworth, and Peckham. It will also give direct access to the Great Western, the North Western Railway, the Great Northern and Metropolitan Railway; thus affording the greatest possible facilities for excursion traffic to the Palace from all parts of the country. With the two latter companies arrangements have been made for running through trains to the Palace from all the stations on their respective systems.

The line must command by far the largest portion of the traffic to the Crystal Palace, and by affording a new and improved route and increased facilities, will doubtless tend to increase that traffic which has never yet been fully developed, owing to the disadvantages of the existing route, and the danger and inconvenience attending the transit by railway on days of great attraction at the Palace.

The remunerative character of the traffic to the Palace, independently of local traffic, may be gathered from the fact that the sum of £150,000 expended on the branch line constructed by the Brighton Company was repaid to them out of receipts in the first three years after the opening of the line.

The value of the local traffic of the particular district is established by the fact that the traffic returns of the Brighton Company between London and Forest-hill, Sydenham, Anerley, Norwood and the Crystal Palace for the six years prior to 1858, increased from £110,000 to £250,000 per annum. Since 1858 there has been a still greater increase.

Under the arrangement made with the London Chatham and Dover Railway Company for working the line, the Crystal Palace and South London Railway Company are to receive out of the gross receipts from traffic booked between the Metropolitan Extension Line of the London Chatham and Dover Railway Company and the Crystal Palace line, as well as the traffic on that line, after deducting working expenses, in no case to exceed 60 per cent, the sum of £34,000 per annum; any excess in receipts above that sum to be divided equally between the two companies.

The subjoined table shows the various metropolitan and suburban stations which will be brought into direct communication with the Palace and the surrounding district.

It is proposed, in pursuance of the Company's Act of Parliament, to raise the capital in 67,500 £10 shares, divided into 33,750 B shares, and 33,750 A shares; the B shares to be entitled to a preference of six per cent in perpetuity over the A shares.

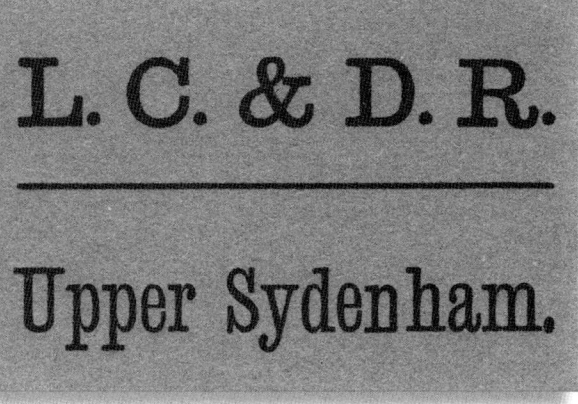

Railway Ephemera

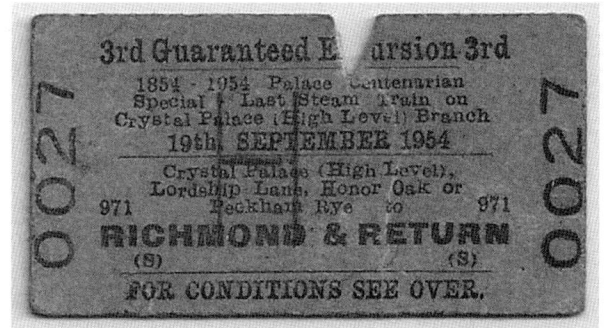

Plates 95, 96 and 97 - Railway companies used a prodigious number of luggage labels, some quite specific as to origin and destination, others less so. To the left is a London, Chatham & Dover example for labelling to Upper Sydenham, whilst the two below have been printed for use by both the South Eastern and the London, Chatham & Dover companies for goods and luggage to Crystal Palace (High Level) & Upper Norwood, the full title of the High Level station. The three labels are actually a blue/green colour, resulting in this tasteful shade of grey when illustrated in monochrome.

Plate 98 - At bottom left is a ticket for the 'Palace Centenarian' special excursion of 19th September 1954, the day after closure of the line to all public traffic.

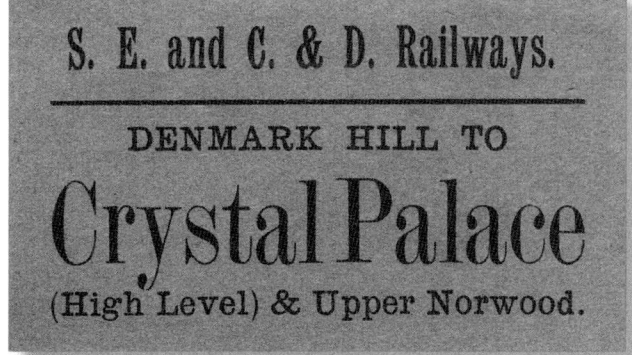

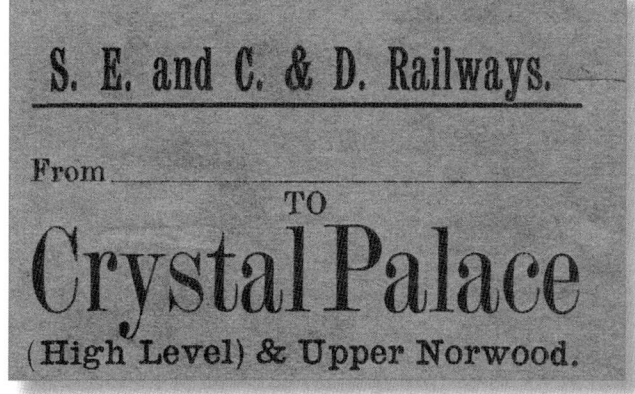

The contractors, Messrs Peto, Betts, and Crampton have agreed to complete the works in two years, and guarantee six per cent on the B shares until 12 months after the opening of the line; so that this capital may be regarded as bearing a permanent dividend of six per cent. The whole of the A shares have been subscribed for, and a considerable proportion of the B shares.

A deposit of £2 10s per share will be payable on or before the 15th June next at the bankers of the Company, and the remainder in calls of £2 10s each, at intervals of three months; or the holders of shares will have the option of paying up in full, and receiving interest at the rate of six per cent per annum upon all payments made in anticipation of calls. The interest account will be made up half-yearly to the 31st December and the 30th June, and the warrants will be issued on the 15th January and 15th July, payable to the bankers of the Company.

Considerably more than one-half of the above shares have already been placed, and applications for the un-issued portion of the six per cent preference B shares may be made to Messrs. Knight, Coleman and Co. the brokers to the Company, 1, Royal Exchange-buildings, London, where authority to the bankers to receive payments in full may be obtained.

———

Metropolitan and Suburban Stations connected with the Crystal Palace :-

From the Crystal Palace to Blackfriars (Surrey side), Ludgate, Farringdon-street, Finsbury-circus, King's-cross (Great Northern), Gower-street, Portland-road, Baker-street, Edgware-road, Paddington, Victoria Station.

From the Palace to Beckenham, Penge, Dulwich, Herne-hill, Forest-hill, Peckham, Denmark-hill, Camberwell-road, Camberwell-gate, Elephant and Castle, Brixton, Clapham, Wandsworth, Battersea.

❄ *Appendix Three* ❄

FIRST NOTICE TO PARLIAMENT

The following is a copy of a notice held in the archives of the Centre for Kentish Studies in Maidstone. The notice concerns the Crystal Palace & South London Junction Railway, and gives details of the sections of railway line to be constructed and the Acts to be amended. It also sets out the working arrangements to be adopted by the London Chatham and Dover Railway for operating the new railway.

In addition to this notice there are two Books of Reference which give details of the land to be purchased, together with plans and sections showing the proposed line of the railway.

———————

Crystal Palace and South London Junction Railway (Incorporation of Company; Construction of Railways; Working and other Arrangements with the London, Chatham, and Dover Railway Company; Amendment of Acts.)

Notice is hereby given, that it is intended to apply to Parliament in the ensuing session for an Act to incorporate a Company for making and maintaining, and to authorise them to make and maintain the railways following, or either of them, with all proper works, communications, and conveniences.

1stly. A railway commencing by a junction with the authorised London, Chatham and Dover Metropolitan Extension Railway (No.3) third junction, in a field numbered 32, in the parish of Saint Mary, Lambeth, on the deposited plan of the said London, Chatham and Dover Metropolitan Extension Railway (No.3) third junction at a point 110 yards to the eastward of Barrington-road, and 45 yards or thereabouts, to the northward of Cold Harbour-lane, and terminating in a piece of ground numbered 26 in the hamlet of Dulwich, parish of Saint Giles, Camberwell, on the deposited plans of the aforesaid London, Chatham, and Dover Metropolitan Extension Railway (No.1) third junction, at a point opposite to, and 88 yards, or thereabouts, distant in a north-westerly direction from the western corner of the Crystal Palace at Sydenham.

2ndly. A railway commencing by a junction with the authorised London, Chatham, and Dover Metropolitan Extension Railway (No.2) in a field numbered 1. x in the parish of Saint Giles, Camberwell, on the deposited plans of the London, Chatham, and Dover Metropolitan Extension aforesaid, at a point 70 yards, or thereabouts, to the north-east of the fence dividing the said field (No.1. x) Saint Giles, Camberwell; from the field (No. 69) in the parish of Saint Mary, Lambeth, on the said plans, and terminating by a junction with the first-mentioned proposed railway, at a point in a field at the back of a house (in the occupation of Mrs Nash) in Denmark Hill, Camberwell, and which point is distant 230 yards, or

thereabouts, to the west of the west end of Champion-park, in the said parish of Saint Giles, Camberwell, which said railways will be made in, from, through, or into the parishes, townships, and extra-parochial places following, or some of them, that is to say: Peckham, Saint Mary, Lambeth, Saint Giles, Camberwell, hamlet of Penge, parish of Saint Mary, Battersea, and Saint Paul, Deptford, Beckenham, Sydenham, and Lewisham, in the county of Kent.

And it is intended by the said Act to make provision for effecting the following objects, or some of them, that is to say: To empower the intended Company to cross, alter, divert, or stop up, either temporarily or permanently, such roads, bridges, highways, footpaths, rivers, aqueducts, streams, canals, navigations, sewers, drains, watercourses, tramways, and passages within the said parishes, townships, and extra-parochial and other places, or some of them, as it may be necessary or desirable to interfere with for the purposes of the said intended railways. To purchase land, houses, and hereditaments by compulsion and by agreement, for the purposes of the said intended railways and works; and to vary, repeal, or extinguish all existing rights and privileges in any manner connected with the lands or hereditaments purchased or taken, or which would in any manner impede or interfere with the construction, maintenance, and use of the said intended railways and works. To confer other rights and privileges; to levy tolls, rates, and charges for and in respect of the use of the said intended railways and works, and to grant exemptions from such tolls, rates, and charges.

To empower the intended Company and the London, Chatham, and Dover Railway Company to enter into and carry into effect contracts and arrangements for or with reference to the construction, maintenance, working, and use by the London, Chatham, and Dover Railway Company of the said intended railways and works, or either of them; the supply and maintenance of engines, carriages, stock, and plant for the same; the collection, regulation, management, and transmission of the traffic thereon; the fixing, collection, payment, division, appropriation, and distribution of the tolls and other incomes and profits arising therefrom, and the employment of officers and servants. To alter (so far as may be necessary for the purposes of the said Bill, or of any such contract or arrangement) the tolls, rates, and duties which the London, Chatham, and Dover Railway Company are now authorised to levy, and to confer, vary, or extinguish exemptions from the payment thereof. To amend (so far as may be necessary for the purposes of the said Bill) the following Acts, viz.: "The East Kent Railway Act 1853;" "The East Kent Railway (Extension to Dover) Act, 1855;" "The Local and Personal Act" (18 and 19 Vict., cap.94), relating to the East Kent Railway Company; "The East Kent Railway (Extension to Dover) Amendment Act, 1857;" "The East Kent Railway (Extension to Dover) Amendment Act, 1858;" "East Kent Railway (Western Extension) Act, 1858;" Local and Personal Act, 22 and 23 Vict., cap.54; 23 and 24 Vict., caps.174, 177, and 187; 24 and 25 Vict., caps.239 and 240.

To empower the London, Chatham, and Dover Railway Company to subscribe towards and become shareholders in the undertaking to be authorised by the said Bill, and to guarantee any dividend or interest on any of the capital raised or borrowed for the purposes thereof, and to appoint directors of the Company.

Plans and sections of the proposed railways and works, a book of reference to such plans, a published map showing the lines of the proposed railways, and a copy of this notice, will, on or before the 30th day of November instant, be deposited for public inspection with the Clerk of the Peace for the county of Kent, at his office in Maidstone, in that county; and with the Clerk of the Peace for the county of Surrey, at his office in Lambeth, in that county; and on or before the 30th day of November instant, a copy of so much of the said plans, sections, and book of reference as relates to each parish or extra-parochial place in or through which the proposed railways and works are intended to be made, with a copy of this notice, will be deposited for public inspection in the case of each such parish which is included in Schedule A to the Public Act 18 and 19 Vict., cap.

120, for the better local management of the metropolis, with the Vestry Clerk of each such parish, at his office; in the case of each such parish or place which is included in Schedule B to that Act, with the Clerk of the District Board of Works, for the district in which such parish or place is comprised, at his office in that district; and in case of each other parish with the Parish Clerk thereof, at his residence; and in the case of each other extra-parochial place with the Parish Clerk of some parish immediately adjoining thereto, at his residence.

Printed copies of the intended Act will be deposited at the Private Bill Office of the House of Commons on or before the 23rd day of December next.

Dated this 8th day of November, 1861.
Fredk. Gale, 43, Parliament Street.

_____

The above notice has the following handwritten annotation added:-

"Deposited with the Clerk of the Peace for the County of Kent this thirtieth day of November one thousand eight hundred and sixty one at five o'clock p.m. by Mr R. E. Diggels for Messrs Freshfields and Newman Solicitors."

Signed by the Clerk of the Peace for the County of Kent
❖

❖ *Acknowledgements* ❖

The archivists at Bromley, Croydon, Southwark, Lambeth, Lewisham and Upper Norwood libraries, and also the staff at the National Archives at Kew, have all been very helpful dealing with my enquiries.

Thanks to Ray Blanchard and Gary Cross of Southwark Model Railway Club, who have been researching the branch for a number of years with a view to building a model of Crystal Palace High Level station, for reading the completed manuscript and for providing contacts and assistance with illustrations.

Thanks are due to to the following for their help: Chantal Morel, Leo Held and Anna Lines (The Norwood Society), Jim Greaves (The South Eastern & Chatham Railway Society), Ken Kiss (The Crystal Palace Museum), John Major (The Dulwich Estate), Hannah Walker (The South London Press), Mike Morant, David Rylands, and staff at the Institution of Civil Engineers. Additional help has been forthcoming from Neil Sprinks, Nick Pomfret, John Nicholas, Maurice Hopper (Historical Model Railway Society), Terry Silcock (Railway Correspondence & Travel Society) and Ray Caston (Signalling Record Society).

I also wish to thank Neil Parkhouse and Tony Miller of Black Dwarf Lightmoor for their invaluable assistance.

44

❈ Notes ❈

Chapter 1 - Paxton's Palace
1. *Cassell's Illustrated History of England*, p.6
2. *South London Society of Architects*, Vol.2 No.9, 20th October 1896
3. *The Times*, 1st December 1936
4. De Maré, Eric, *The Year of The Great Exhibition*, p.99
5. Ibid., p.102
6. The National Archives, RAIL 414/1
7. *Journal of the Crystal Palace Foundation*, Summer 1994, p.12
8. *Handbook of the Crystal Palace*, April 1935
9. *Cassell's Illustrated History of England*, p.162
10. Warwick, Alan R., *The Phoenix Suburb*, p.97
11. Biddle, G., *Victorian Stations*, p.209
12. Warwick, Alan R., *The Phoenix Suburb*, p.97
13. *Southern Railway Magazine*, January 1937
14. *The Times*, 12th June 1854
15. Corbet Anderson, J., *The Great North Wood*, pp.57-58
16. Jackson, A. A., *London's Local Railways*, p.101
17. Measom, G., *The Official Illustrated Guide to the Brighton and South Coast Railway and its branches*
18. Ruskin, J., *The opening of the Crystal Palace considered in some of its relations to the Prospects of Art*
19. *Journal of the Crystal Palace Foundation*, Winter 1991/2, p.5
20. Howard Turner, J. T., *The London, Brighton & South Coast Railway*, p.265

Chapter 2 - The Birth of the Crystal Palace & South London Jct Railway
1. Jackson, A. A., *London's Local Railways*, p.101
2. Ibid.
3. Moody, G. T., *Railway World*, October 1954, p.227
4. Minutes of Estates Governors Executive Committee meeting 4th January 1862
5. Ibid.
6. Ibid.
7. *British Railway Journal*, No.28 Autumn 1989, p.354
8. Minutes of Estates Governors Special Executive Committee meeting, 9th January 1862
9. *Platt's Handbook to the Crystal Palace District*, p.50
10. Davies, E., *The Book of Dulwich*, p.23
11. *British Railway Journal*, No.28 Autumn 1989, p.354
12. I.C.E Minutes of Proceedings, Vol.50 1877
13. *British Railway Journal*, No.28 Autumn 1989, p.355
14. The National Archives, RAIL 146/2
15. *South London Chronicle*, 7th June 1862
16. Bromley Local Studies Library
17. Gray, A., *The London, Chatham & Dover Railway*, p.181
18. I.C.E. Minutes of Proceedings, Vol.107 1892
19. *Sydenham & Penge Gazette*, 10th August 1912
20. I.C.E Minutes of Proceedings, Vol.107 1892
21. Ibid.
22. The National Archives, RAIL 146/2
23. *British Railway Journal* No.28 Autumn 1989, p.355
24. Minutes of Estates Governors Executive Committee meeting, 26th November 1863
25. The National Archives, RAIL 146/2
26. Minutes of Estates Governors Executive Committee meeting, 12th January 1864
27. The National Archives, RAIL 146/2
28. Goode, C. T., *To the Crystal Palace*, p.19
29. *South London Chronicle*, 20th February 1864
30. *Croydon Times*, 4th September 1864
31. *Railway Magazine*, November/December 1946
32. *Croydon Times*, 26th November 1864
33. The National Archives, RAIL 146/2
34. Biddle, G., *Victorian Stations*, p.210
35. *Illustrated London News*, 30th September 1865

36. The National Archives, RAIL 146/2
37. *British Railway Journal* No.28 Autumn 1989, p.356
38. The South Eastern & Chatham Railway Society
39. *Illustrated London News*, 30th September 1865
40. Goode, C. T., *To the Crystal Palace*, p.20
41. *The Croydon Chronicle*, 1st April 1865
42. Gray, A., *The London, Chatham & Dover Railway*, p.141
43. Ibid., p.146
44. *Norwood Review & Crystal Palace Reporter*, 27th December 1884
45. Ibid., 6th December 1884
46. *Sydenham & Penge Gazette*, 11th January 1890
47. *South London Press*, 5th August 1865
48. *Croydon Times*, 30th August !865
49. *Railway World*, 1954
50. The National Archives, RAIL 146/2
51. Whyler, T*he Development of the Railway System in the Bromley Area 1839-1923*
52. *Mercury Connection*, p.27, Southwark Local Studies Library
53. Kidner, R. W., *The London, Chatham & Dover Railway*, pp.12-13, 31-32
54. Ibid.
55. *British Railway Journal* No.28 Autumn 1989, p.356
56. Ibid.
57. *Sydenham & Penge Gazette*, 21st June 1873
58. *South Eastern & Chatham Railway Society Journal*, 1984
59. *South London Press*, 22nd December 1866
60. Dyos, H. J., *Victorian Suburb*, p.72
61. Jackson, A. A., *London's Local Railways*, p.103
62. Ibid.
63. *South London Press*, 11th September 1869
64. *Norwood News*, 15th August 1868 & 19th December 1868
65. The National Archives, RAIL 635/200, Petition initiated by Bridge Street Chapel, Greenwich
66. *Norwood News*, 1899
67. Lambeth Council Minutes, General Purposes Committee, 28th February 1962

Chapter 3 - The London, Chatham & Dover takes over
1. *South London Press*, 1st September 1866
2. Ibid., 31st August 1867
3. The National Archives, RAIL 146/2
4. *South London Press*, 9th October 1869
5. *Norwood News*, 10th June 1871
6. *Crystal Palace, Penge, Upper Norwood Directory* 1874/75 Croydon Local Studies Library
7. The National Archives, RAIL 146/4
8. Kidner, R. W., *The London, Chatham & Dover Railway*, p.13
9. *Norwood News*, 29th June 1872
10. Ibid., 27th July 1872
11. *Sydenham & Penge Gazette*, 12th August 1876
12. Ibid.
13. *Norwood News*, 28th December 1872
14. The National Archives, RAIL 146/4
15. Gray, A., *The London, Chatham & Dover Railway*, p.145
16. *British Railway Journal* No.28 Autumn 1989, p.361
17. Bromley Local Studies Library
18. Williams, R. A., *The London & South Western Railway*, Vol.1 pp.229-230
19. *Sydenham & Penge Gazette*, 5th April 1873
20. Williams, R. A., *The London & South Western Railway*, Vol.1 pp.229-230
21. Gray, A., *The London, Chatham & Dover Railway*, pp.187-189
22. *Norwood Review & Crystal Palace Reporter*, 16th March 1889
23. Ibid., 15th December 1888
24. Prochaska, F. K., *Women & Philanthropy in 19th Century England*, pp.5, 224
25. Ibid.
26. *Norwood News*, 19th June 1942

27   *Norwood Review & Crystal Palace Reporter*, 9th August 1884
28   *Sydenham & Penge Gazette*, 17th September 1879
29   *Norwood Review & Crystal Palace Reporter*, 5th October 1889
30   Ibid., 4th May 1889
31   *Norwood News*, 10th June 1871
32   Ibid.
33   *Norwood Review & Crystal Palace Reporter*, 7th February 1880
34   Ibid., 10th July 1886
35   Ibid., 30th July 1887
36   *Sydenham & Penge Gazette*, 7th December 1878
37   *Norwood Review & Crystal Palace Reporter*, 12th November 1887
38   *Norwood News*, 7th September 1872
39   Parliamentary Papers 1841, Vol.VIII Q784
40   *The Railway Traveller's Handy Book*, p.81
41   *Norwood Review & Crystal Palace Reporter*, 30th December 1882
42   Ibid., 31st May 1884
43   Ibid., 28th May 1881
44   Ibid., 30th November 1889
45   Kidner, R. W., *The London, Chatham & Dover Railway*, pp.36-37
46   *Norwood Review & Crystal Palace Reporter*, 18th December 1886
47   *Sydenham & Penge Gazette*, 21st November 1891
48   *Norwood Review & Crystal Palace Reporter*, 13th December 1884
49   Ibid., 11th August 1888
50   *Sydenham & Penge Gazette*, 5th November 1890
51   Ibid., 27th September 1890
52   *Norwood Review & Crystal Palace Reporter*, 7th June 1884
53   Ibid., 2nd June 1888
54   Pullen, Doris E., *Forest Hill*, p.48
55   *Cassell's Illustrated History of England*, Vol.VIII p.22
56   *Norwood Review & Crystal Palace Reporter*, 8th March 1884
57   Ibid., 7th February 1880
58   Ibid., 16th January 1886
59   Ibid., 9th February 1889
60   Ibid., 4th September 1886
61   Ibid., 25th June 1887
62   Course, Edwin, *Victorian Railways*, p.257
63   Searle, Muriel V., *Lost Lines*, p.51
64   *Norwood Review & Crystal Palace Reporter*, 20th August 1885
65   *Sydenham & Penge Gazette*, 5th November 1892
66   *Norwood Review & Crystal Palace Reporter*, 8th October 1881
67   Ibid., 4th June 1881
68   Ibid., 6th September 1884
69   Ibid., 10th August 1889
70   Ibid., 1st January 1887
71   Ibid., 9th February 1889
72   *Sydenham & Penge Gazette*, 29th November 1890, 6th December 1890
73   Ibid., 28th July 1895
74   *Norwood News*, 27th May 1893
75   *Sydenham & Penge Gazette*, 26th June 1895
76   Ibid., 18th May 1895
77   *Norwood News*, 9th December 1893
78   *Norwood Review & Crystal Palace Reporter*, 25th September 1886

Chapter 4 - The South Eastern & Chatham Railway
1   *Norwood Review & Crystal Palace Reporter*, 28th February 1880
2   Ibid., 18th August 1881
3   Ibid., 3rd March 1883
4   Ibid., 10th March 1883
5   Ibid., 13th September 1884
6   Ibid., 14th October 1882
7   Ibid., 7th October 1882
8   *Sydenham & Penge Gazette*, 27th April 1895
9   Mercury Connection, *British Rail & The Mercury Group*, p.27
10   Gray, A., *The London, Chatham & Dover Railway*, p.17
11   *South Eastern & Chatham Railway Society Journal*, 1984
12   *Sydenham & Penge Gazette*, 23rd February 1922
13   *British Railway Journal* No.28 Autumn 1989, p.363
14   Kidner, R. W., *The London, Chatham & Dover Railway*, p.36
15   *Sydenham & Penge Gazette*, 31st August 1901
16   Ibid., 9th February 1901
17   Ibid., 18th June 1904

18   Ibid., 21st September 1901
19   Ibid., 10th March 1900
20   Ibid., 19th August 1905
21   Ibid., 25th December 1909
22   Ibid., 1st July 1911
23   Ibid., 12th April 1902
24   Ibid., 17th May 1902
25   Ibid., 28th January 1909
26   Ibid., 2nd October 1909
27   *Norwood News*, 7th June 1913
28   Ibid., 1st November 1913
29   *Sydenham & Penge Gazette*, 10th May 1902
30   Ibid., 30th August 1902
31   *British Railway Journal* No.28 Autumn 1989, p.363
32   Moody G. T., 'The Crystal Palace (High Level) Line' *Railway World*, October 1954, p.228
33   *Sydenham & Penge Gazette*, 17th January 1903
34   Ibid., 31st January 1903
35   Ibid., 17th January 1903
36   *Norwood News*, 23rd September 1906
37   *Sydenham & Penge Gazette*, 10th February 1912
38   Ibid., 30th September 1911, 26th August 1911
39   Ibid.
40   *Trains Illustrated* Vol.VII October 1954, p.433
41   The South Eastern & Chatham Railway Society
42   Hamilton J. A. B., *Britain's Railways in World War I*, p.49
43   *British Railway Journal* No.28 Autumn 1989, p.363
44   *Norwood News*, 29th December 1916
45   Ibid.
46   Ibid., 15th December 1916
47   Ibid., 5th January 1917
48   Ibid., 7th March 1919
49   *British Railway Journal* No.28 Autumn 1989, p.363
50   *Norwood News*, 4th July 1919
51   Nock O. S., *The South Eastern & Chatham Railway*, p.162

Chapter 5 - The Southern Railway
1   *Trains Illustrated* Vol.VII October 1954, p.433
2   *South London Press*, 27th August 1920
3   *Norwood News*, 9th September 1921
4   Ibid., 13th October 1922
5   Ibid., 19th August 1921
6   Ibid., 21st March 1924
7   Ibid., 1st December 1922
8   *Sydenham & Penge Gazette*, 5th January 1923
9   Ibid., 23rd February 1923
10   Simmons, Jack, *The Railways of Britain*, pp43-44
11   *Sydenham & Penge Gazette*, 5th January 1923
12   *Norwood News*, 6th November 1923
13   Ibid., 12th December 1924
14   *Sydenham & Penge Gazette*, 9th January 1925
15   *British Railway Journal* No.28 Autumn 1989, p.363
16   Moody G. T., *Southern Electric*, pp.28, 36
17   *Sydenham & Penge Gazette*, 10th July 1925
18   Ibid., 20th March 1925
19   Moody G. T., *Southern Electric*, pp.28
20   *Sydenham & Penge Gazette*, 12th June 1925
21   Ibid., 10th July 1925
22   Moody G. T., *Southern Electric*, pp.28
23   *Sydenham & Penge Gazette*, 14th August 1925
24   *British Railway Journal* No.28 Autumn 1989, p.367
25   Simmons, Jack, *The Railways of Britain*, p.155
26   *Norwood News*, 22nd January 1927
27   Ibid., 14th September 1923
28   Ibid., 12th July 1929
29   Ibid., 28th December 1928
30   Ibid., 19th February 1932
31   Ibid., 15th May 1931
32   Ibid., 25th March 1932
33   *Sydenham, Forest Hill and Penge Gazette*, 10th August 1934
34   Ibid.

35   *Norwood News*, 1st January 1932
36   Ibid., 5th July 1935
37   Ibid., 31st January1936
38   Ibid., 20th November 1936
39   The Crystal Palace Foundation, *The Crystal Palace is on fire*, p.49
40   Jackson, Alan A., *London's Local Railways*, p.111
41   'The Crystal Palace Fire - The Stationmaster's Story', *Southern Railway Magazine*, January 1937
42   Ibid.
43   *Norwood News*, 30th April 1937
44   Ibid., 23rd April 1937
45   Ibid., 17th February 1939
46   Ibid., 9th December 1938
47   *Southern Railway Magazine*, March 1939
48   *Norwood News*, 8th March 1940
49   Ibid., 16th February 1940
50   Jackson, Alan A., *London's Local Railways*, p.111
51   *Norwood News*, 28th April 1944
52   Ibid., May 1944
53   *British Railway Journal*, No.28 Autumn 1989, p.377,
54   *Trains Illustrated* Vol.VII October 1954, p.435
55   *Norwood News*, May 1944
56   Ibid., 27th October 1944
57   Ibid., 3rd November 1944
58   Ibid., 9th February 1945
59   Ibid., 28th January 1944
60   The National Archives, AN 2/235 (604/113/2)
61   Ibid.
62   Ibid.
63   Ibid.
64   Ibid.
65   *Norwood News*, 17th August 1945
66   Jackson, Alan A., *London's Local Railways*, p.111
67   *Norwood News*, 30th April 1948
68   Moody G. T., *Southern Electric*, p.147
69   *Norwood News*, 31st May 1946
70   *British Railway Journal*, No.28 Autumn 1989, p.381
71   *Norwood News*, 24th May 1946
72   Ibid., 7th March 1947
73   Ibid., 3rd October 1947
74   Lambeth Council Minutes, General Purposes Committee, 26th February 1947
75   Festival Handbook 1951, Norwood Library Archives
76   *British Railways Southern Region Magazine*, December 1948
77   Simmons, Jack, *The Railways of Britain*, p.52-53
78   Ibid.

Chapter 6 - Final Closure

1   *Norwood News*, 8th July 1949
2   Clayton, Antony, *Subterranean City*, p.159
3   *Norwood News*, 29th July 1949
4   *Railway World*, October 1954
5   *Norwood News*, 11th November 1949
6   The National Archives, AN 13/1787
7   *Trains Illustrated* Vol.VII October 1954, p.435
8   *Norwood News*, 10th July 1953
9   Ibid., 29th January 1954
10   Ibid., 5th March 1954
11   The National Archives, AN 177/240
12   The National Archives, AN 13/1787
13   Ibid.
14   Ibid.
15   Ibid.
16   Camberwell Council Minutes, Finance Committee, 17th March 1954
17   The National Archives, AN 13/1787
18   Ibid. and *Norwood News*, 18th June 1954
19   The National Archives, AN 174/71
20   The National Archives, AN 13/1787
21   *Norwood News*, 23rd July 1954
22   Ibid., 13th August 1954
23   Ibid., 15th August 1954

24   Ibid.
25   *British Railway Journal*, No.28 Autumn 1989, p.381
26   *Norwood News*, 24th September 1954
27   *The Croydon Advertiser*, Week ending 25th September 1954
28   *The Daily Herald*, 20th September 1954
29   *British Railway Journal*, No.28 Autumn 1989, p.381
30   *The Norwood Society* 1979
31   *Norwood News*, 24th September 1954
32   *The Daily Herald*, 20th September1954
33   *British Railway Journal*, No.28 Autumn 1989, p.381
34   Turner, R. C., *Black Clouds & White Feathers*, p.181
35   *The Times*, 20th September 1954
36   *Norwood News*, 12th November 1954
37   *The Croydon Advertiser*, 28th March 1968
38   Ibid., week ending 16th March 1957
39   *South London Press*, 26th August 1960
40   Ibid.
41   *Beckenham Journal*, 15th October 1981
42   *Norwood News*, 12th March 1961
43   *The Croydon Advertiser*, 20th August 1961
44   *West Norwood & District News*, 21st July 1967
45   *The Croydon Advertiser*, 12th December 1968
46   GLC - Housing Development Committee, 14th July 1977
47   *Norwood News*, 15th May 1953
48   *South London Press*, 3rd August 1973
49   *The Times*, 14th May 1977
50   'Green Walk along the old Crystal Palace (High Level) railway' - Friends of the Great North Wood
51   Henshaw, D., *The Great Railway Conspiracy*, p.51
52   The National Archives, AN 13/1787
53   Searle, Muriel V., *Lost Lines*, p.54
54   The National Archives, AN 174/71
55   *South London Press*, 7th March 1950
56   Lambeth Council Minutes, General Purposes Committee, 22nd March 1950
57   Henshaw, D., *The Great Railway Conspiracy*, p.88
58   Ibid.
59   'Pruning the Branch Lines', *British Railways Magazine*, February 1954
60   Warwick, Alan R., *The Phoenix Suburb*, p.96

❈ *Bibliography* ❈

Biddle, G., *Victorian Stations*, David & Charles 1973

Cassell's Illustrated History of England, London, Cassell & Company Ltd

Clayton, Antony, *Subterranean City*, London, Historical Publications Ltd 2000

Corbet Anderson, J., *The Great North Wood*, published 1898

Course, Edwin, *Victorian Railways*, Lewisham Local Studies Library

Davies, E., *The Book of Dulwich*, Barracuda Books 1975

De Maré, Eric, *The Year of the Great Exhibition*, London, The Folio Society 1972

Dyos, H. J., *Victorian Suburb*, Leicester University Press 1961. Reproduced by kind permission of Continuum Publishing Group

Goode, C. T., *To the Crystal Palace*, Bracknell, Forge Books 1984

Gray, A., *The London, Chatham & Dover Railway*, Rainham, Meresborough Books 1984

Hamilton, J. A. B., *Britain's Railways in World War I*, George Allen & Unwin Ltd 1967

Henshaw, D., *The Great Railway Conspiracy*, Leading Edge Press & Publishing Ltd 1991

Howard Turner, J. T., *The London, Brighton & South Coast Railway*, London, B.T. Batsford Ltd

Jackson, A. A., *London's Local Railways*, David & Charles 1983

Kidner, R. W., *The London, Chatham & Dover Railway*, The Oakwood Press 1952

Measom, G., *The Official Illustrated Guide to the LBSCR and its Branches*, London, Waterflow & Sons

Moody, G. T., *Southern Electric*, Ian Allan Publishing 1979

Nock, O. S., *The South Eastern & Chatham Railway*, Ian Allan Ltd 1961

Prochaska, F. K., *Women & Philanthropy in 19th Century England*, Oxford, Clarendon Press 1980

Pullen, Doris E., *Forest Hill*, published 1979

The Railway Traveller's Handy Book, published 1862, reprint Adam & Dart 1971

Ruskin, J., *The Opening of the Crystal Palace: Considered in some of its relations to the Prospects of Art*, London, Elder & Co. 1854

Searle, Muriel, V., *Lost Lines*, New Cavendish Books 1982

Simmons, Jack, *The Railways of Britain*, London, Macmillan Publishers Ltd 1986

Turner, R. C., *Black Clouds & White Feathers*, Ian Allan Publishing 1989

Warwick, Alan R., *The Phoenix Suburb*, Southampton, The Blue Boar Press 1973

Whyler, *The Development of the Railway System in the Bromley Area 1839-1923*, Beckenham Library

Williams R. A., *The London & South Western Railway* Vol.I, Ian Allan 1968

❈

❖   *Other Sources of Information*   ❖

Primary Sources

The National Archives: RAIL 414/1, RAIL 146/2, RAIL 635/200, RAIL 146/4, AN 2/235 (604/113/2), AN 13/1787, AN 177/240, AN 174/71

Minutes of Estate Governors, Alleyn's College of God's Gift: 4th January 1862, 9th January 1862, 26th November 1863, 12th January 1864 (The Old College, Dulwich, SE21 7AE)

Camberwell Council Minutes - Finance Committee, 17th March 1954

GLC Housing Development Committee, 14th July 1977

Institution of Civil Engineers - Minutes of Proceedings, Vol.50 1877, Vol.107 1892

Lambeth Council Minutes - General Purposes Committee, 26th February 1947, 22nd March 1950

Parliamentary Papers 1841, Vol.VIII, Q784 (Middlesex University Library)

Newspapers

The Times, London

Beckenham Journal

The Croydon Chronicle

Croydon Times

The Croydon Advertiser

The Daily Herald

Illustrated London News

Mercury Connection

Norwood News

Norwood Review & Crystal Palace Reporter

South London Chronicle

South London Press

Sydenham & Penge Gazette

West Norwood & District News

Periodicals

British Railway Journal No.28, Autumn 1989

British Railways Magazine, February 1954

Journal of the Crystal Palace Foundation, Winter 1991/2, Summer 1994

Railway World, 1954

Railway Magazine, November/December 1946

Southern Railway Magazine, January 1937

South London Society of Architects, Vol.2 No.9, 20th October 1996

The South Eastern & Chatham Railway Society, web page

Trains Illustrated, Vol.VII, October 1954

British Railways Southern Region Magazine

The Norwood Society Journal, 1979

❖